The Egyptian Food Subsidy System

Structure, Performance, and Options for Reform

Akhter U. Ahmed

Howarth E. Bouis

Tamar Gutner

Hans Löfgren

Research Report 119

International Food Policy Research Institute
Washington, D.C.

Library of Congress Cataloging-in-Publication Data

The Egyptian food subsidy system : structure, performance, and options for reform / Akhter U. Ahmed . . . [et al.].
p. cm. — (Research report / International food Policy Research Institute ; 119)
Includes bibliographical references.
ISBN 0-89629-121-9
1. Food relief—Egypt. 2. Food relief—Egypt—Costs. 3. Subsidies—Egypt. I. Ahmed, Akhter U. II. Research report (International Food Policy Research Institute) ; 119

HV696.F6 E37 2001
363.8′82′0962—dc21 2001024291

Contents

Tables

Figures

Foreword

In the early 1980s, Egypt spent a substantial part of its national budget on subsidies for a dozen different rationed foods. The costs of the subsidies were rapidly becoming unsustainable. The Government of Egypt asked IFPRI to study the effectiveness of its food subsidy system and to look at ways to reduce costs without jeopardizing the welfare of the poor. Several IFPRI research reports were published as an outcome of this research (see Research Report 34, *Egypt's Food Subsidy and Rationing System: A Description,* and Research Report 45, *The Effects of the Egyptian Food Ration and Subsidy System on Income Distribution and Consumption*).

As a result of the strategies Egypt has undertaken since the late 1980s, the cost of the food subsidy has fallen from 14 percent of total government expenditures in 1980/81 to less than 6 percent in 1996/97. Nevertheless, costs remain high (about US$1.1 billion in 1996/97). Because many policymakers are concerned that further efforts to cut costs and reform the system might threaten the food security of those who need it most, the Government of Egypt again asked IFPRI to conduct food policy research in collaboration with Egypt's Ministry of Agriculture and Land Reclamation and Ministry of Trade and Supply over a three-year period beginning in 1996.

This report is one result of comprehensive research evaluating key performance indicators of the system. It finds that the current food subsidy system generally does a good job in providing food security for the poor, but much of the subsidized food also reaches those who are relatively well off. Tighter targeting of food subsidies could make the system more efficient without increasing costs prohibitively.

This work in Egypt adds to an extensive body of past research on food subsidies and food security for the poor in a number of countries including Bangladesh, Pakistan, and the Philippines. Work is also under way in a number of other countries, particularly in Africa.

Per Pinstrup-Andersen
Director General

Acknowledgments

Between 1996 and 1999, IFPRI, in collaboration with the Egyptian government's Ministry of Agriculture and Land Reclamation (MALR) and Ministry of Trade and Supply (MOTS), conducted the research that underpins this report on food security issues in Egypt. We gratefully acknowledge the U.S. Agency for International Development (USAID) for funding the Food Security Research Project in Egypt under USAID Grant Number 263-G-00-96-00030-00. We are particularly indebted to David Alverson, Craig Anderson, Thomas Olson, Mohamed Omran, Glenn Rogers, and Fenton Sands of the Economic Growth/Agricultural Policy Division at USAID Egypt for their advice and support.

The Food Security Research Project was one of the units of the Agricultural Policy Reform Program (APRP) in Egypt. We are grateful to Saad Nassar, director, and the members of the Program Planning Committee of APRP, particularly Hamdy Salem and Mahmoud Nour, for their guidance. Our thanks also go to the members of other APRP units, and especially to Gary Ender, Lehman Fletcher, and John Holtzman for their useful comments and suggestions on earlier versions of this report. We also thank the concerned officials from MALR and MOTS for their cooperation.

Our research in Egypt was a collaborative effort with many Egyptian experts and researchers. We are especially grateful to Ali Abdel Rahman Ali, Sonia Ali, Abdel-Razek Hassan Abdel-Razzek, Salwa Gomaa, Shafika Nasser, Nagla Salem, and Gamal Siam for their contribution in conducting the research in Egypt. We also thank enumerators and supervisors from MALR and MOTS who helped us implement the Egypt Integrated Household Survey.

The study would not have been possible without the dedication and hard work of the staff in the IFPRI Cairo office, who facilitated various aspects of our research and project administration. Our special thanks go to Dawoud Al-Husseini, Ahmed Qadry Bahloul, Asmaa El-Ganainy, Amina Hegazy, Nelly Shaheen, Ayman Tawfik, and Maged El Wakkad.

At IFPRI, we thank the director of the Food Consumption and Nutrition Division, Lawrence Haddad, who was also director of the Food Security Research Project in Egypt, for his stimulating comments and suggestions on this report, and for his overall guidance. Thanks also go to Gaurav Datt, Dean Jolliffe, Manohar Sharma, Jay Willis, and Yisehac Yohannes for their input to this study.

We thank Mark Rosegrant for coordinating the review of this report. We benefited from the helpful and valuable comments from the three reviewers: Mylène Kherallah, Joachim von Braun, and an anonymous reviewer. We are also grateful for the editorial assistance of Uday Mohan and Phyllis Skillman.

Summary

Egypt's food subsidy system has been a mainstay of the government's long-term policy of promoting social equity and political stability. It has also been a major component of the social safety net for the poor, guaranteeing the availability of affordable staples, helping to reduce infant mortality and malnutrition, and mitigating the adverse effects of recent economic reform and structural adjustment. The cost of the system has declined considerably from 14 percent of government expenditures in 1980/81 to 5.6 percent in 1996/97. The absolute cost, however, remains high: In 1996/97, the total cost was 3.74 billion Egyptian pounds (LE) or about US$1.1 billion. The government and various stakeholders agree that the system's costs can be further reduced and its efficiency improved with better targeting to the needy.

The Egyptian Food Subsidy System: Structure, Performance, and Options for Reform evaluates the economic, political, and technical feasibility of reducing costs while improving or maintaining the welfare of the poor. The report addresses five questions: (1) How well does the present system target the poor? (2) How much leakage—the pilferage of subsidized foods in the distribution channel—occurs? (3) At what cost does the government transfer income to the needy? (4) How can subsidies be better targeted to the needy? and (5) What are politically feasible options for reform?

The subsidy system includes four foods: *baladi* bread, wheat flour, sugar, and cooking oil. *Baladi* bread and wheat flour are available to consumers of all income levels without restrictions. Sugar and cooking oil are targeted—they are available only to those with ration cards. In principle, higher-income households should get low-subsidy red ration cards and lower-income households should get high-subsidy green cards.

Targeting the Needy

The present system does not target the poor as well as it should. Subsidy benefits are about equally distributed across income groups: 1 percent of the population receives more or less 1 percent of the benefits. This distribution pattern is quite similar to the one of the early 1980s and reveals that the majority of benefits accrue to the nonneedy. Poor targeting combined with system leakage led to only about one-third of the subsidy going to the needy. Of this, *baladi* bread accounted for 65 percent; wheat flour, 13 percent; sugar, 12 percent; and cooking oil, 10 percent.

Baladi bread and wheat flour accounted for about 77 percent of the subsidy in 1997. The untargeted system for these goods allows all consumers to benefit, but is an expensive way to improve the food security and nutrition of the poor.

Sugar and cooking oil subsidies are not well targeted. A majority of the wealthy households (about 71 percent of households in the top three quintiles) carry the high-subsidy green ration cards. These households receive about 62 percent of the rationed subsidy benefits. On the other hand, about 10 percent of needy households hold the low-subsidy red cards, and about 14 percent of poor households have no card of any kind.

Food subsidies can be better targeted to the poor. For this to occur, the following measures are needed:

1. *Baladi* bread distribution outlets should be concentrated in poor neighborhoods. Currently in urban areas, the number of *baladi* bread outlets in wealthy neighborhoods is greater per capita than in poor ones.
2. Rural areas and other areas where poverty is concentrated should receive higher shares of total food subsidies. A strong urban bias exists in the allocation of subsidies across Egypt. According to the 1996 census, 57 percent of the population lived in rural areas, but only 30 percent of food subsidies were allocated to these areas in 1996/97. Moreover, governorate-level allocations do not consider the geographic distribution of poverty.
3. The ration card system for sugar and oil should provide high-subsidy green cards only to low-income households and convert the green cards of non-needy families to low-subsidy red cards.
4. The government should mix maize flour with *baladi* wheat flour at flour mills. Intermediaries would not then be able to sift the mixed flour to separate the higher quality wheat flour to sell at market prices.
5. A proxy means test, which relies on indicators highly correlated with household income, should be applied to distinguish poor from non-poor households.

Leakage and Cost-Effectiveness

Considerable leakage occurs because the subsidies create a strong incentive for intermediaries to sell subsidized foods illegally at market prices. Twenty-eight percent of subsidized wheat flour leaked in this way, 20 percent of sugar, 15 percent of cooking oil, and 12 percent of *baladi* bread.

Overall, the government spends LE 3.06 to transfer LE 1.00 of income to a needy household through the food subsidy system. The cost of transferring LE 1.00 to general consumers of *baladi* bread is LE 1.16. But because 61 percent of the benefit from the *baladi* bread subsidy goes to the non-needy, the cost of reaching a needy household increases to LE 2.98. At LE 4.64, the cooking-oil subsidy is the least cost-effective in directing LE 1.00 of income to the needy. The costs of transferring LE 1.00 of benefits to needy consumers through the sugar and wheat flour subsidy system are LE 3.34 and LE 3.71, respectively.

The current *baladi* bread subsidy provides a relatively effective means of transferring benefits to the poor, particularly the urban poor, helping to protect them against shocks that may arise from the ongoing economic reform process in Egypt.

Practical Reforms

A number of reforms are administratively and politically feasible. Because there is no pressing need for far-reaching change, government officials and various stakeholders believe that extreme measures such as increasing the *baladi* bread price to eliminate the subsidy or targeting bread subsidies by using food stamps or coupons are unrealistic. The feasible reforms can be divided into two groups, based on the degree of political opposition they would probably encounter. Policies that would likely meet little opposition include revamping the ration card system by decreasing rationed food subsidies for the non-needy, and mixing maize flour with *baladi* wheat flour at the milling site to reduce leakage. Options that would engender greater opposition are eliminating the sugar and oil subsidies, targeting bread outlets to poor neighborhoods, and reallocating supplies to the governorates according to their poverty levels. The losses the non-needy would incur from these reforms do not appear to be large. Therefore, these options are feasible if the political will exists to implement them.

CHAPTER 1

Introduction

The food subsidy system in Egypt—which presently covers *baladi* bread, *baladi* flour, cooking oil, and sugar—has been effective as a major component of Egypt's social safety net helping to protect the poor. Other components of the safety net include other consumer subsidies (water, energy, housing, education, health, and transportation), social insurance, cash transfers, microcredit programs, and activities financed by the Social Fund for Development, which was set up in 1991 to mitigate the adverse effects of structural adjustment on the poor.

The food subsidy system is widely credited with guaranteeing the availability of affordable staples to the population and helping to reduce infant mortality and malnutrition (World Bank 1995). However, any household in Egypt has the option of participating in the food subsidy system. Such general, nontargeted programs can incur large costs to the government. Alternative policies and programs may be more cost-effective in helping the poor. But even if such alternatives can be identified, some influential groups may receive fewer benefits than under the present system, so that it may be politically difficult to implement such alternatives.

At the request of the Government of Egypt, IFPRI conducted policy research on food security issues in Egypt over a three-year period starting in 1996, in collaboration with the Ministry of Agriculture and Land Reclamation (MALR) and the Ministry of Trade and Supply (MOTS). This study is an outcome of that research.

The overall objectives of this study are to evaluate the performance of Egypt's food subsidy system and to examine the economic, political, and technical feasibility and efficacy of a variety of strategies for reforms that reduce costs but maintain or even improve the welfare of the poor. It is hoped that this analysis will serve the dual purposes of assisting the Egyptian government in improving the efficiency of the present system, while adding significantly to the knowledge base on food subsidy systems and reforms in developing countries in general.

Food subsidy costs in Egypt have declined to about 5 percent of government expenditures in recent years from a high of 14 percent in 1981/82. Nevertheless, their absolute costs remain high, totaling 3.7 billion Egyptian pounds (LE) in 1996/97 in current prices.[1] In comparative terms, this expenditure roughly corresponds to total earnings from tourism, or 58 percent of the revenue generated by the Suez Canal in the same year. Moreover, subsidy costs are vulnerable to increases in international wheat prices. Indeed, Egypt is one of the world's top importers of wheat, importing just under 50 percent of total wheat consumption.[2] At present, about 85 percent of all wheat imports are channeled through the food subsidy system. Because *baladi* bread and wheat flour account for more than 75 percent of subsidy costs, government officials are aware that unanticipated price shocks in commodities such as wheat could immediately change the impact of food subsidy costs on the overall government budget.

Food subsidies are perceived to be important in promoting political stability in Egypt. Sharp increases in the prices of food staples and other products in 1977 ignited riots in Egypt that were seen as a threat to government stability. These riots left a legacy of government caution regarding strategies for reforming food subsidy, in order to avoid policy changes that may be a focus for discontent. Similar riots over the past 15 years in other countries in the region, such as Jordan, Morocco, Tunisia, and Yemen, have also reinforced this emphasis on gradualism.

Since food subsidy expenditures reached unsustainable peaks in the early 1980s, the Egyptian government has employed a number of gradual policy steps to reform the system. It has made tremendous progress in this effort and has done so without political unrest. The challenge it currently faces is whether and how to reform the system further to better target subsidies and therefore bring greater benefits to the poor, while working in a more efficient and cost-effective manner. In assessing options for policy reform, the government is aware of the importance of balancing the economic benefits and costs of different policy options with their political and social benefits and costs. In particular, options for food subsidy policy reform must be considered within the context of the far-reaching economic reform and structural adjustment programs that the government has pursued since 1991. These reforms have brought significant macroeconomic benefits, but they have also heightened the government's desire to insulate the poor and others adversely affected by the reform process.

Subsidized *baladi* bread and wheat flour are intended to be available to all households, although participation may be limited by the proximity of an outlet, and the willingness to wait in line to make a purchase.[3] An untargeted food subsidy program has the advantage of maximum coverage of the population without requiring government bureaucracy to identify people who are eligible for subsidy benefits. How-

---

[1] The exchange rate in 1997 was Egyptian pounds (LE) 3.40 to US$1.00.

[2] According to U.S. Department of Agriculture data, Egypt was the world's top importer of wheat and wheat flour in 1997/98 and was the second largest importer in 1996/97 (USDA 1999).

[3] Recently the government has closed all subsidized wheat flour warehouses in the metropolitan areas of Cairo, Alexandria, Suez, and Port Said.

ever, because it provides benefits to the nonneedy as well as the needy, an untargeted food subsidy program can be an expensive way to improve food security and the nutritional status of the poor.

In contrast to *baladi* bread and flour subsidies, rationed sugar and oil subsidies are explicitly designed to be targeted. Lower-subsidy *red* ration cards are intended for people who earn higher incomes, and higher-subsidy *green* ration cards are intended for the poor. But some wealthier Egyptians carry the higher-subsidy green ration cards, while some of the poorest families hold red cards or no ration card at all.[4] It seems likely that there is scope for improvement in the distribution of benefits from the ration cards.

Another factor reducing the effectiveness of the subsidy system in providing benefits to the poor is leakage. Leakage is defined in this study as the amount of subsidized foods that do not reach the consumer—that is, which disappear in the distribution channel. One of the questions that this report addresses is how much leakage is occurring and where?

The remaining eight chapters of the report are organized as follows. Chapters 2 through 4 are descriptive, providing the policy context and describing how the bulk of the information used in Chapters 5 through 8 was gathered. Chapter 2 reviews the economic and political context of food subsidy reform in Egypt since World War II, in order to highlight some of the major factors that shape the feasibility of different options for reforming the subsidy system. Chapter 3 describes the operation and the structure of the present food subsidy system. Chapter 4 discusses the nationally representative household and community surveys conducted by IFPRI, primary data that are the basis for most of the empirical analysis. Secondary data obtained from MOTS, the Central Agency for Public Mobilization and Statistics (CAPMAS), and various other published sources are also used. In addition, the political analysis of policy options is based, in part, on structured interviews with policymakers at the central government and governorate level, and with major domestic stakeholders, major donors, and academics.

Chapters 5 and 6 address specific topics related to the evaluation of the operation of the food subsidy system. These include an analysis of allocation of subsidized foods to 26 governorates and household participation in the food subsidy system by income group by urban and rural areas (Chapter 5). This information then provides the background and basis for measuring and understanding, in Chapter 6, the degree of leakage of food subsidies, how well food subsidies are targeted to the poor, and the cost-effectiveness of the present food subsidy system in reaching the poor.

Chapter 7 provides an overview of overall food demand patterns and develops estimates of consumer responses to price and income changes. Chapter 8 examines

[4] The government is keen to improve targeting of ration cards and is currently considering steps to rectify the present distribution, that is to "clean" the ration card system. One of the major obstacles it has faced in its efforts to improve targeting is development of a "means test" that is inexpensive to administer and that also accurately identifies poor and nonpoor households. The IFPRI research on this topic is reported in Chapter 9.

multiple options for reforming the existing subsidy system and uses a Computable General Equilibrium (CGE) model of Egypt to simulate the impact of selected policy options. Chapter 9 summarizes the findings and conclusions concerning options for reform of the food subsidy system. Finally, Appendixes A to E describe various aspects of the methodology and data collection in detail. Appendix F presents supplementary tables.

CHAPTER 2

The Policy Context

The Egyptian government's involvement in consumer food subsidies started as early as the years following World War I, when the government responded to rising food prices by importing large quantities of wheat and flour from Australia and selling it at a loss in government-owned shops in 1919/20 (Scobie 1981). Since World War II, Egypt's food subsidy system has gone through two main phases: the growth of the system to unsustainable levels by the early 1980s and since then, the gradual contraction of the system to its current levels. This contraction has been undertaken quietly, without much publicity, given the political sensitivity of food subsidies in Egypt, particularly with respect to *baladi* bread.

Over time, subsidized bread has become a powerful symbol of the broader social contract between the Egyptian government and the population. Since the Nasser era (1952–70), the state has made explicit its mandate to ensure basic food supplies for Egyptians (Khouri-Dager 1996). As Singerman (1995) has noted, "The Egyptian Government's policies of political exclusion have gone hand in hand with their public commitment to provide for the basic needs of the population. Because it limits and controls mass participation, the government maintains its legitimacy by providing goods and services to the population." This chapter places Egypt's food subsidy policies in a historical context, in order to highlight the political and economic considerations that have shaped them.

Historical Background

Food rationing began as a temporary measure in Egypt in 1941, designed to help Egyptians cope with scarcity and inflation resulting from World War II. The initial system was not targeted to the poor but was set up to provide everyone with necessities such as sugar, kerosene, coarse cotton textiles, edible oil, and tea (Ali and Adams 1996). Following President Gamal Abdel Nasser's "July Revolution" in 1952, agrarian reforms marked the beginning of extensive government involvement in the production, marketing, and distribution of most agricultural products, which lasted until the start of liberalization of state agriculture in 1987 (Badiane, Kherallah, and Abdel-Latif 1998).

The food subsidy system expanded in the 1960s and 1970s, becoming part of a broader set of consumer welfare programs that also subsidized transport, housing, energy, water, health, education, and some nonfood consumer products, such as soap and cigarettes. These policies reflected the government's desire to hold consumer prices down in the face of urbanization and rapid population growth.

In the mid-1960s, ration cards were introduced for a small number of goods in response to rising domestic prices and shortages, caused in part by the discontinuance of U.S. food aid at the time of the 1967 Arab-Israeli War (Alderman, von Braun, and Sakr 1982).[5] As a result, Egypt was forced to use foreign exchange reserves to pay for imports, and food shortages resulted in rising food prices.

The ration cards initially did not involve price subsidies, but were designed as a quantity rationing system to help ensure that all Egyptians would be shielded against commodity shortages. Indeed, consumer subsidies were reduced at the time of the 1967 war, in order to cut back on Egypt's need for imported goods (Scobie 1981). In general, under President Nasser, spending on food subsidies remained a modest percentage of the government's budget, and the primary role of food subsidy policies was to ensure the supply of essential food items.

Wheat imports began exceeding domestic production in 1963, and at its nadir in 1983, Egypt was producing less than 20 percent of its wheat needs (Scobie 1981; Badiane, Kherallah, and Abdel-Latif 1998). As a result of declining per capita domestic wheat production and growing demand for wheat, Egypt became increasingly dependent on wheat imports from the mid-1960s to the mid-1980s. Starting in 1987, however, the government embarked on a series of agricultural reforms. With these reforms, both area planted to wheat and wheat yields increased dramatically, which resulted in a tripling of wheat production from the early 1980s to the mid-1990s. Higher production, however, has only kept pace with growing consumption: since the mid-1980s, wheat import requirements have remained at 6–7 million metric tons per year (Badiane, Kherallah, and Abdel-Latif 1998).

Expansion of Food Subsidies

The food subsidy system grew significantly in scope and cost under President Anwar Sadat, who took power in 1970. A broader set of foods was brought under the subsidy umbrella, including beans, lentils, frozen fish, meat, and chicken, as well as rice and yellow maize. At its peak, the subsidy system included 18 foods.

Food security became a major policy issue in Egypt in 1972, as world wheat prices skyrocketed from \$60 to \$250 a ton in U.S. dollars by 1973, and the cost of Egypt's wheat imports surged from \$147 million to \$400 million (Sadowski 1991). Overall, expenditures on food subsidies jumped from LE 3 million in 1970/71 (only 0.2 percent of total government expenditure) to LE 1.4 billion in 1980/81, which accounted for 14 percent of total government expenditure (Alderman 1982).

---

[5] These included tea, kerosene, oil, and sugar.

The 1977 Riots

The infamous 1977 riots deeply unnerved Egyptian policymakers and left a legacy of government caution not only toward food policy reform, but economic reform more broadly. The riots illustrate all of the strategies policymakers should avoid in reforming food subsidy policy, that is, high, sharp price increases in a political context where the public perceives the changes to be inequitable (Seddon 1986). Although the riots are commonly termed "food riots," they were in fact "equity riots," since the underlying issues had more to do with the perception that the policy change was unfair, rather than the actual policy change itself (Alderman 1991). Indeed, the price increases announced in January 1977 did *not* include increases in a number of subsidized staples, such as *baladi* bread, beans, lentils, rationed sugar, or cooking oil. Price increases were announced for *fino* bread (50 percent) and for 72 percent-extraction flour from which *fino* bread is made (67 percent), as well as for regulated sugar (4 percent), rationed rice (20 percent), tea (subsidy canceled), *butagas,* the butane gas used for cooking, (46 percent), gasoline (26–31 percent), and cigarettes (different amounts) (Alderman 1986). The subsidy cuts stemmed from negotiations between the government and the International Monetary Fund (IMF) in 1976 over a package of economic reforms for the economy. Subsidy cuts were part of the package, although the actual policies that sparked the riots were more modest than those the IMF initially proposed (Sadowski 1991). Egyptians were angry about the subsidy cuts, since the government had promised that Sadat's "Open Door Economic Policies" would result in greater prosperity for everyone, and that subsidies on basic commodities would remain intact (Gutner, Gomaa, and Nasser 1998).

Rioting flared up in various places along the Nile Valley, but mainly in Cairo and Alexandria. The violence, however, ended only when the government backed down and rescinded the subsidy cuts on January 20, 1977. After the 1977 riots, Sadat further expanded the subsidy system to increase the value of existing subsidies and to extend the distribution of flour from urban areas to rural areas (Sadowski 1991). This move reflected his interest in placating the public and countering criticism that his government was not doing enough to promote social equity. Food subsidies came to be seen as both a safety net to protect the poor and an important tool in the promotion of social equity.

Reduction Phase

The subsidy system was becoming increasingly unsustainable by the late 1970s and early 1980s as demand for subsidized wheat and bread increased, and growing wheat imports left Egypt more vulnerable to swings in international wheat prices and supply. Wheat is the foundation of the Egyptian diet, and subsidized bread and flour accounted for more than half (53.7 percent) of total food subsidy expenditures at its peak in 1980/81 (Table 2.1).

When President Hosni Mubarak took office in 1981, he was faced with the daunting task of easing the acute economic burden imposed by the food subsidy system.

Table 2.1—Total explicit subsidy costs of Egypt's food subsidy system, by commodity, 1980/81 to 1996/97

Year	Bread	Wheat flour	Sugar	Cooking oil	Other commodities[a]	Total food subsidies	Total food subsidies[b]	Total government expenditure	Food subsidies as percentage of total government expenditure
			(LE million in nominal terms)				(LE million in real terms)	(LE million in nominal terms)	(percent)
1980/81	618.7	147.4	141.2	76.7	443.3	1,427.3	5,266.8	10,250	13.9
1981/82	633.1	155.0	95.7	76.1	662.0	1,621.9	5,984.9	12,260	13.2
1982/83	596.0	142.9	62.2	46.4	563.6	1,411.1	4,451.4	14,645	9.6
1983/84	544.4	97.6	46.1	133.1	878.8	1,700.0	4,657.5	16,232	10.5
1984/85	526.8	100.3	59.5	166.6	774.5	1,627.7	4,238.8	18,277	8.9
1985/86	557.8	104.6	117.3	129.0	659.9	1,568.6	3,902.0	24,285	6.5
1986/87	538.1	97.3	176.3	52.5	462.3	1,326.5	2,902.6	24,530	5.4
1987/88	578.5	99.8	255.8	37.4	142.8	1,114.3	2,142.9	33,460	3.3
1988/89	460.7	164.1	378.0	48.5	264.8	1,316.1	2,136.6	33,400	3.9
1989/90	698.0	250.4	516.0	47.7	315.4	1,827.4	2,503.3	34,230	5.3
1990/91	612.5	377.4	509.3	160.0	333.9	1,993.0	2,386.9	50,390	4.0
1991/92	928.7	495.8	583.5	367.9	106.7	2,482.6	2,482.6	50,963	4.9
1992/93	1,026.1	546.9	507.3	276.9	. . .	2,357.2	2,144.8	52,223	4.5
1993/94	1,322.6	241.0	149.5	243.3	. . .	1,956.4	1,663.6	56,264	3.5
1994/95	1,328.7	174.8	209.3	349.2	. . .	2,061.9	1,602.1	58,526	3.5
1995/96	1,945.6	305.8	310.6	402.5	. . .	2,964.4	2,111.4	63,889	4.6
1996/97	2,307.8	558.6	489.5	384.7	. . .	3,740.6	2,517.2	66,826	5.6

Sources: Bread, wheat flour, sugar, and cooking oil subsidy costs were calculated by authors from unpublished data, Ministry of Trade and Supply. Subsidy costs for other commodities were also obtained from the Ministry of Trade and Supply. Total government expenditure data were obtained from the Ministry of Finance and the Ministry of Trade and Supply.

Notes: Ellipsis (. . .) indicates commodities removed from the subsidy program.

[a] Other commodities include maize, rice, lentils, chicken, frozen fish, and frozen meat.

[b] Total food subsidies in real terms were calculated by deflating nominal costs by GDP deflator (1991/92 = 100).

In 1982, he initiated a process of reforming the food subsidy system, which he launched by holding a conference on national economic issues to seek the advice of prominent Egyptian officials, businessmen, and intellectuals (Sadowski 1991). There was agreement at this conference that Egypt's persistent budget deficits must be tackled in order to reduce inflation and high levels of foreign borrowing. In addition, rising subsidy costs were seen as a key contributor to the deficit problem. During this period, and over the next decade, Mubarak's advisers developed several strategies to gradually reform the subsidy system. The broad approach they adopted was a slow transformation of the system as a means to avoid political protest. This approach, according to senior Egyptian officials involved in its development, was based on the assumption that the most important obstacle to subsidy reduction was public perception, and if change were introduced gradually, people would not perceive that their living standards were being sharply reduced (Sadowski 1991). The government's specific strategies since the early 1980s have included

1. Attempts to better target the ration card system by introducing in 1981 red ration cards, which offer a lower subsidy on goods such as sugar, cooking oil, tea, and rice than the existing green card. The red cards are intended for people in higher-income jobs.
2. A reduction in the number of subsidized foods. Meat, chicken, fish, and other foods mainly consumed by higher-income groups were removed from the subsidy program. Subsidies on meat were removed in 1990/91, those on fish and tea in 1991/92, and those on rice in October 1992.
3. Reductions in the number of people on the ration card system. These were cut back from 99 percent in the early 1980s to around 70 percent in 1998. In 1989, MOTS stopped adding newborns to the ration card system. Other reduction strategies included canceling cards owned by people who had died or moved abroad.
4. A slow reduction in subsidies through various techniques, such as gradually reducing the quantity of a particular subsidized food, in some cases gradually replacing it with a more expensive version. An example of this is the increase in the price of bread from 1 piaster to 2 piasters in 1984, without protest. The government's strategy was to introduce a higher-quality 2 piaster loaf alongside the 1 piaster loaf.[6] Over time, the old loaf became harder to find and its quality had deteriorated. Finally, the 1 piaster loaf was no longer produced, but most people switched to the widely available 2 piaster version without complaint (Sadowski 1991). Using the same strategy, the government further increased bread prices to 5 piasters in 1989, also without protest.

Other examples of this quiet reform process for *baladi* bread include decreases in loaf size (from 168 grams to 160 grams in 1984 and to 130 grams in 1991), and

[6] Some outlets would offer higher-quality bread and other outlets lower-quality bread. That is, it was not possible for consumers to choose between the two types at the same outlet.

more recently, the addition of maize flour in some areas. The government also ended subsidies on *fino* bread and 72 percent-extraction flour in 1992 and on *shami* bread and 76 percent-extraction flour in 1996.

The result of these policy steps has been a significant reduction in the number of subsidized foods and a decline in subsidy costs in real terms from a peak of almost LE 6.0 billion in 1981/82 to LE 2.5 billion in 1996/97 in constant 1991/92 prices (Table 2.1). The current food subsidy system covers only four food items: *baladi* bread, *baladi* flour, cooking oil, and sugar. The explicit cost of food subsidies has fallen from 13.9 percent of total government expenditures in 1980/81 to 5.6 percent of such expenditures in 1996/97 (Table 2.1). Before the exchange rate was unified in Egypt in 1991/92, explicitly subsidized foods also received large implicit subsidies, because the government imported food and other commodities at an overvalued exchange rate. According to World Bank calculations, implicit food subsidies accounted for 39.4 percent of total food subsidies (explicit plus implicit) and 2.8 percent of the gross domestic product (GDP) in 1989/90 (World Bank 1995).

Gradual liberalization of wheat input and output markets since 1987 has resulted in a dramatic increase of domestic wheat production, which tripled between the early 1980s and 1995. While Egypt is still one of the world's largest importers of wheat, its self-sufficiency has improved significantly in the past decade, to just under 50 percent by 1995 (Badiane, Kherallah, and Abdel-Latif 1998). Despite these improvements, there is still significant scope for further improvement in the food subsidy system, particularly by improving targeting and reducing leakage, which are discussed in subsequent chapters.

Economic and Political Dynamics of Subsidy Reform

Egypt began a substantive process of economic reform and structural adjustment in 1991, backed by agreements with the World Bank and the IMF. The goal of the economic reform and structural adjustment program was to promote economic growth—and therefore to reduce unemployment and poverty—by creating a market-based, export-oriented economy. The result of the program has been a significant improvement in Egypt's macroeconomic performance.

Despite the positive economic results brought about by the economic reform process, domestic support for the process among various political parties and social groups has been mixed. Sociopolitical unrest—as indicated by demonstrations, strikes, and riots, and violent attacks—did increase sharply in the early 1990s, compared with previous years, coinciding with the implementation of the structural adjustment and economic reform programs (Ibrahim and Lofgren 1996; Clarke 1997).

Currently in Egypt there is near consensus among major domestic political actors that food subsidies are an important social safety net, but one that can be improved to better target the poor. President Mubarak has stressed numerous times that bread subsidies will not be removed, while at the same time playing the leading role in initiating the process of reforming the subsidy system that began in the early 1980s. The ruling National Democratic Party, in turn, has called for better targeting of food subsidies since the late 1980s. Egypt's other political parties, while not grass-roots organizations and without direct power, are mainly opposed to any removal of subsidies, but some have recommended a greater "rationing" of subsidies to reduce leakage and waste (Gutner, Gomaa, and Nasser 1998).[7]

At the same time, there is little external pressure on Egypt to undertake a dramatic reform of its food subsidy system. This conclusion, based on interviews with Egypt's major donors and analysis of policy documents (often confidential) highlighting donors' strategies in the country, is somewhat counterintuitive, in the sense that there is a perception among many domestic stakeholders that external pressure for subsidy reform is prevalent (Gutner, Gomaa, and Nasser 1998).

In terms of the politically sensitive issue of *baladi* bread and flour, no major donors are calling for the abolishment of subsidies or an increase in prices. Donors do support measures to better target the system to the poor while reducing its cost, which are in line with the interests of the two ministries (MALR and MOTS). They are also aware that while Egypt's macroeconomic climate has improved, unemployment has increased, and there is also a widespread belief that social conditions must be improved.

At the same time, donors have pushed for food subsidy reform in the past, and may reexamine the issue as Egypt's economy becomes healthier. However, donor leverage has historically been mixed in Egypt; that is, what donors want and what they are able to achieve are not always the same (Zimmerman 1993; Clarke 1997; Cassandra 1995).

Of the major donors, the United States Agency for International Development (USAID) has been more active than most in promoting better-targeted food subsidies, as a component of its Agricultural Policy Reform Program. One of the program's goals is to target food subsidies to the poorest households. USAID officials in Cairo acknowledged that while there was donor pressure on the country to cut back on food subsidies in the early 1990s, by the mid-1990s the issue was less pressing, given the improving health of the Egyptian economy.[8] In addition, in the early 1990s, USAID was keen on the idea of encouraging Egypt to set up a targeted food subsidy system—such as one using food stamps or coupons. This idea also lost some of its urgency a few years later, given the perception that such a policy reform was politically unacceptable.[9] USAID officials have said that USAID's current goal is to help Egypt improve the efficiency of its food subsidy program in ways that safeguard the poor but are also more cost-effective.[10]

The IMF is also a highly influential donor institution in Egypt, in part because its standby agreements have been necessary for Egypt to receive World Bank loans, and

[7] Only one party, the Liberal (Al Ahrar) party, called for the complete removal of subsidies during the 1987 elections. However, more recently, it has maintained a more moderate position calling for better targeting, rather than abolishment.

[8] Author interviews with USAID officials, Cairo, Egypt, May 3 and 5, 1998.

[9] Author interviews with USAID officials, Cairo, Egypt, May 3 and 5, 1998.

[10] Author interviews with USAID officials, Cairo, Egypt, May 3 and 5, 1998.

more recently, compliance with IMF and World Bank stabilization measures has been necessary for the 1992 and 1994 reductions in debt owed to the Paris Club group of Western creditor countries (Amin 1995). Food subsidy reform appeared as a component of the 1991 IMF program, as one of many measures to help reduce the government budget deficit. However, the necessity of addressing food subsidies has declined in importance, and the most recent standby agreement—covering the period October 1996–September 1998—did not mention food subsidy reform.

A third major donor in Egypt is the World Bank, and its strategies have been relatively modest compared with the United States or IMF. World Bank average annual lending commitments to Egypt in the period FY95–97 averaged $110 million, down from $375 million in 1992. In addition, Egypt's access to International Development Association (IDA), the Bank's soft-lending arm, is being phased out after 1999, given the country's access to other forms of external financing and its per capita income of around $1,060. Because the World Bank's leverage, based on financial contributions, is "severely limited" in Egypt, the Bank has emphasized its contribution to Egypt's development through its nonlending services, such as analytical assistance and policy advice (World Bank 1997).

The World Bank's focus in Egypt is to help support the government's goal of reducing unemployment and increasing living standards. Food subsidy issues in Egypt are not a direct area of World Bank work, but it has noted that improvements in Egypt's social safety net are important in the country's war on poverty.

In summary, at present, there is relatively limited political pressure for reforms in a significantly slimmed-down food subsidy system. Nevertheless, about US$1.1 billion is currently spent annually by the government on the food subsidy system, which could be allocated to help the poor in other ways. Subsequent chapters explore the extent to which the present system helps the poor and alternatives for reform to reduce government costs and improve targeting to help the poor.

CHAPTER 3

How the Present Food Subsidy System Operates

In 1996/97, the total cost of Egypt's food subsidy system was LE 3.74 billion (see Table 2.1), of which *baladi* bread accounted for 61.7 percent; wheat flour, 14.9 percent; sugar, 13.1 percent; and cooking oil, 10.3 percent.[11] The rates of subsidy to consumers per unit of commodity are shown in Table 3.1.

The General Authority for Supply Commodities (GASC), an agency of MOTS, is the government agency that absorbs most of the food subsidy costs through its budget. The government obtains wheat both from the international market and from local production. The GASC is responsible for all imports of subsidized wheat, which it undertakes through international tenders and long-term bilateral contracts.[12]

The Principal Bank for Development and Agricultural Credit (PBDAC), whose activities are coordinated by MALR and supervised by the Central Bank, is responsible for purchasing wheat from local farmers for the subsidy system under the domestic wheat procurement program. This wheat is processed both in government-run mills and private mills contracted by the government. Since 1989/90, private millers also have been permitted to purchase wheat directly from farmers to produce 82 percent-extraction wheat flour for use in the food subsidy system.

Sugar from domestic production is supplied to the subsidy system through the Food Industries Holding Company (FIHC), an agency of the Ministry of Public Enterprises. Subsidized sugar comes entirely from domestic production. The GASC makes payments to the PBDAC, wheat flour mills, and the FIHC for the domestic supplies of wheat and sugar that enter the food subsidy system.

In the case of cooking oil, the FIHC both imports and procures oil from domestic production, which is then turned over to the GASC without payment. The GASC collects the proceeds from the sales of cooking oil at a subsidized price to ration

---

[11] Appendix A describes the method used to estimate the cost of the food subsidy system and, as an example, calculates the cost for the *baladi* bread subsidy system in 1996/97.

[12] There are some private imports of wheat.

Table 3.1—Rates of food subsidy to consumers per unit of commodity, 1996/97

Subsidized foods	Full cost[a]	Subsidized price	Rate of subsidy
	(LE)	(LE)	(percent)
Baladi bread (per loaf)	0.12	0.05	56.9
Wheat flour (per kilogram)	0.97	0.55	43.1
Sugar (per kilogram):			
Green card (fully subsidized)	1.32	0.50	62.1
Red card (partially subsidized)	1.32	0.75	43.2
Edible oil (per kilogram):			
Green card (fully subsidized)	2.18	1.00	54.1
Red card (partially subsidized)	2.18	1.25	42.7

Sources: Calculated by the authors from unpublished data provided by the Ministry of Trade and Supply, and data for baking costs of *baladi* bread taken from the community survey component of the "Egypt Integrated Household Survey, 1997," undertaken for IFPRI's Food Security Research Project in Egypt.

[a] Full costs are calculated by adding costs of internal transportation, storage, handling, milling, and baking (for bread) to c.i.f. import prices. Rate of subsidy is the difference between the full cost and subsidized price, divided by full cost.

(*tamween*) shops and then transfers the revenue to the Ministry of Finance. As a result of this structure, the GASC's budget does not bear the cost of subsidizing cooking oil.

In 1997/98, 77.4 percent of all subsidized wheat was imported. Historically, the share of imported wheat in the subsidy system has been even higher (Appendix F, Table F.1), but it has been gradually declining in recent years. Although some cooking oil used in the food subsidy system is domestically produced, the bulk of it, 89.8 percent in 1997/98, was imported (Appendix F, Table F.2). Imports are mostly in the form of semi-refined or crude oil, which is refined locally. Since 1991/92, all subsidized sugar has been procured from domestic production (Appendix F, Table F.3). The following sections discuss the structure and operation of each of the subsidized foods in more detail.

Subsidized Bread

Subsidized *baladi* bread is available without restriction to all consumers living in Egypt. The fixed price of *baladi* bread is currently 5 piasters per loaf throughout the country, and no official limits are set on the quantity or frequency of purchases at this price. The price of *baladi* bread has been unchanged since 1989, when it was 2 piasters per loaf.

Consumers normally buy *baladi* bread from outlets run by local municipalities. These outlets are located either inside or close to bakeries. There are 10,693 bakeries in Egypt making *baladi* bread, and virtually all of them (96 percent) are privately owned. Most of the bakeries (71 percent) are located in urban areas (Appendix F, Table F.4). In 1996/97, these urban bakeries received 82 percent of the total amount of subsidized wheat flour allocated to all bakeries; rural bakeries received the remainder.

In 1996/97, a total of 4,669,680 metric tons of subsidized wheat flour (82 percent extraction) was supplied by MOTS, of which 73.2 percent was distributed to bakeries to produce subsidized *baladi* bread and the remainder was distributed to consumer warehouses for distribution as subsidized wheat flour. Bakers receive their subsidized wheat flour in the form of a daily quota of sacks; they pay LE 14.50 for a 50-kilogram sack of flour (that is, LE 290.00 per metric ton). Bakers are required to produce 10 loaves of *baladi* bread per kilogram of flour. Each loaf of baked *baladi* bread is expected to average 130 grams in weight (after water and other ingredients are added).

The local municipality sales outlet selling *baladi* bread receives a commission of LE 1.00 per 1,000 loaves of bread sold. The baker, in turn, receives the sales proceeds after deducting the outlet commission. These proceeds, after subtracting production costs such as the purchase of subsidized flour and other ingredients and baking costs, are intended to provide a "normal" profit margin.

In 1996/97 *baladi* flour was sold to bakeries at a price that was about 70 percent below the full cost to the government. To guard against leakage at the bakery level, officials from MOTS monitor the production of subsidized *baladi* bread. Fines and jail sentences are commonly issued to those bakers who (1) fail to produce the required number of loaves of *baladi* bread, (2) bake underweight loaves of *baladi* bread, or (3) increase the moisture content of *baladi* bread.

Subsidized Wheat Flour

With the exception of the four metropolitan governorates (Cairo, Alexandria, Port Said, and Suez), warehouses for *baladi* wheat flour (82 percent extraction) are located in all governorates, and this wheat flour is, in principle, available to all consumers without restriction.[13] In 1996/97, a total of 1,253,640 metric tons of wheat flour was distributed to consumer warehouses. Consumers purchase subsidized wheat flour directly from warehouses, usually in a 25-kilogram sack.

Currently, there are 20,996 warehouses in Egypt, and they are all privately run. Seventy-two percent are located in rural areas and the rest are in nonmetropolitan urban areas. In 1996/97, rural warehouses received 73 percent of the total quantity of subsidized wheat flour allocated to all warehouses in Egypt. Subsidized wheat flour is sold to warehouses at LE 520 per metric ton, around 80 percent higher than the price of the subsidized flour sold to bakeries. Consumers pay a fixed price of 55 piasters per kilogram, or LE 550 per metric ton.

[13] The government, in fact, is in the process of phasing out wheat flour subsidies. This phase-out started with metropolitan governorates because only a small percentage of city dwellers bake bread at home. This percentage is much higher in rural areas.

Subsidized Sugar and Cooking Oil

Sugar and cooking oil are distributed on a monthly quota basis to consumers through ration cards (*betaka tamween*). In 1996/97, 590,000 metric tons of subsidized sugar and 220,000 metric tons of subsidized oil were supplied to outlets. Consumers holding ration cards buy subsidized sugar and oil at outlets *(tamweens)* located in private groceries that also sell nonsubsidized consumer goods. The *tamweens* are registered by MOTS to receive rations from government wholesale companies operated by the ministry. Ration card holders register their cards with the grocer of their choice. The grocer records monthly purchases of sugar and oil on the card, which has space for recording purchases over a full decade.

It is the responsibility of the card holder to report changes in family size to local offices run by MOTS. However, in 1989, MOTS stopped registering newborn children for the ration system. Deaths or migration of family members must be reported. As a result of these and other measures, coverage of the population under the ration system has fallen from 91.6 percent in 1986/87 to 69.2 percent in 1996/97.

In 1981, in an effort to reduce subsidy costs, MOTS divided all ration card holders into two categories: fully subsidized (green cards) and partially subsidized (red cards). People with higher incomes were assigned to the partially subsidized program. However, from the outset, the number of participants in the partially subsidized program has been very small, accounting for only about 7 percent of the total number of participants in the ration system in 1996/97. All government employees are entitled to hold green ration cards.

The monthly quota for subsidized cooking oil varies between regions. Currently, in metropolitan Cairo, Alexandria, coastal cities, and the frontier governorates, the per capita monthly quota is 500 grams, while it is 300 grams in all other parts of the country. Oil is sold at a price of LE 1.00 per kilogram to green card holders. Red card holders pay LE 1.25 per kilogram of oil. The private market price for cooking oil of similar quality was about LE 3.50 in 1996/97.

For sugar, the monthly quota per capita is 1 kilogram, which is uniform throughout the country. Subsidized prices per kilogram of sugar are LE 0.50 for green card holders and LE 0.75 for red card holders. The private market price for sugar of similar quality was about LE 1.60 in 1996/97.

CHAPTER 4

Household Surveys and Other Information Sources

The analyses of the performance of the Egyptian food subsidy system presented in subsequent chapters are primarily based on data collected in household and community surveys planned and conducted by IFPRI in 1997 in collaboration with MALR and MOTS. These surveys provide key information, otherwise unavailable. They match the characteristics of households (for example, their income level and geographic location) with the extent to which the households use and benefit from the food subsidy system. Community-level surveys were also undertaken in conjunction with the household surveys in order to understand how local services and infrastructure influence use of the food subsidy system. Additional secondary data were obtained from MOTS, CAPMAS, and various other published and unpublished sources.

The political analysis of policy options is based, in part, on structured interviews with policymakers at the central government and governorate levels, and with major domestic stakeholders, donors, and academics. This chapter describes how the household surveys, community surveys, and structured interviews with policymakers and stakeholders were conducted and their content.

Egypt Integrated Household Survey

From March to May 1997, IFPRI, together with MALR and MOTS, carried out the Egypt Integrated Household Survey (EIHS). This was a single-round, nationally representative survey that included urban and rural households. The EIHS collected information on multiple topics, including income, expenditures, food consumption, nutrition and health status, education, employment, rural credit and savings, farming, housing, maternity history, child care, remittances and transfers, migration, and the use of the food subsidy system by households. The survey was administered by a team of male and female interviewers who completed separate male and female questionnaires for each household. The male interviewer questioned a male member of the household, usually the head, and the female interviewer questioned a female household member, typically the wife of the head of the household.

The questionnaires were administered to 2,500 households[14] from 20 governorates (the 6 frontier governorates were excluded), using a two-stage, stratified selection process. The 1986 Egypt census frame and a 1993 listing of households, supplied by CAPMAS, were used for the sample frame. CAPMAS uses this sample frame as a master sample for much of its survey work. The frame consists of 492 primary sampling units, of which 296 are urban and 196 are rural.

Households were selected from the master sample in a two-stage process. In the first stage, 125 primary sampling units were randomly selected with probability proportional to size from the CAPMAS master sample. In the second stage of the process, 20 households were randomly selected from each primary sampling unit. The two-stage process has the advantage over a pure random sample process in that it dramatically reduces the number of primary sampling units to be visited and therefore reduces survey costs. The disadvantage is that standard errors resulting from two-stage samples tend to be significantly higher than those resulting from pure random samples. The design also stratified selection for the following five regions of Egypt: metropolitan, lower urban, lower rural, upper urban, and upper rural.[15]

Much of the household-level analysis in this report aggregates the regional estimates. The EIHS regional samples of households are not self-weighted. Therefore, it is necessary to use weights for any estimates aggregated over regions. These weights are the ratio of the expected number of households in each region if the regional samples were self-weighted, and the actual number of sample households in that region. The regional weights are as follows: metropolitan, 1.3829; lower urban, 0.9456; lower rural, 1.0692; upper urban, 0.8527; and upper rural, 0.7637.

With a nationally representative EIHS sample, it is possible to examine average characteristics of the households at the national level as well as at the regional level. (For more information on the EIHS, including more details on the sample design, strata weights, and fieldwork, see Datt, Jolliffe, and Sharma 1998.)

Community Survey

In June 1997, IFPRI conducted a community survey (a subcomponent of the larger EIHS) to provide primary data for the evaluation of community-level variables. This survey was conducted in communities where respondents from the EIHS households resided. A total of 125 urban and rural communities (corresponding to the 125 primary sampling units sampled in the EIHS) from 20 governorates were surveyed.

[14] Although the EIHS included 2,500 households, 148 households had to be dropped from the analysis because of missing or incomplete data. This report is based on data from 2,352 households, 1,078 of which are classified as urban and 1,274 classified as rural.

[15] This regional classification for Egypt has often been used in the tabulation of data from the Household Income and Expenditure Surveys conducted by CAPMAS.

The community surveys were carried out by EIHS supervisors. In rural areas, the community survey collected information on population characteristics, infrastructure, and access to facilities (this information was obtained from a village counselor); land cultivation patterns, irrigation, crop cycles, and wages (from a local agricultural cooperative officer); microfinance and other development programs (from persons in local government units and other institutions); informal financial markets (from a village counselor); subsidized foods (from the local *tamween* office of MOTS); operation of *baladi* bread bakeries (from bakery owners); and on markets and prices through spot market checks. In urban areas, the community survey covered only a subset of the above information: subsidized foods (from local *tamween* offices), operation of *baladi* bread bakeries, and markets and prices.

Structured Interviews with Policymakers and Stakeholders

Structured one-on-one interviews were undertaken with policymakers at national and governorate levels and with academics and officials from Egypt's major donor agencies (Gutner, Gomaa, and Nasser 1998). The primary objective was to elicit the viewpoints of the actors who would be involved in making policy changes and of elites and others on the political efficacy of a range of policy options for food subsidy reform. As part of this process, IFPRI cosponsored, with Cairo University's Public Administration Research and Consultation Center, a workshop of stakeholders, held June 28, 1998. The workshop was attended by Egypt's Minister of Trade and Supply, Ahmed Goueli, as well as officials from different ministries, members of Parliament, opposition party leaders, and scholars.

CHAPTER 5

The Geographic Allocation and Household-Level Use of Food Subsidies

How does the government allocate food subsidies in each of Egypt's 26 governorates? And how do households use and derive benefits from the food subsidy system? Overall, the urban bias one finds in a number of developing countries is evident in Egypt. The geographical allocation of subsidies is biased toward urban areas, and governorates where proportionately fewer poor reside receive a larger-than-warranted share. This finding is mirrored in the demand-side analysis. This chapter first analyzes regional patterns of subsidy allocation and subsidy benefits and then turns to household use of the food subsidy system. The analysis suggests that there is considerable scope for better targeting of food subsidy benefits to the poor and points out the particular importance of subsidized *baladi* bread vis-à-vis the other three subsidized foods.

Administrative System of Allocations

Given the Egyptian government's objective of reforming the food subsidy system to better target the poor, it is important to understand how the present system of government food subsidy distribution works. Each year, representatives from MOTS (which has overall responsibility for management of the food subsidy system), MALR, the Ministry of Finance, GASC, the Ministry of Public Enterprises, and PBDAC form a program committee that determines the quota of subsidized foods that is to be delivered to each governorate. The committee's assessment is based on an annual Needs Plan, which is essentially calculated by extrapolating past usage based on population growth. This rule of thumb, however, does not necessarily take into consideration the changes in economic conditions in specific governorates (or perhaps even the baseline conditions).

Distribution committees in each governorate, in turn, provide local input into the preparation of the annual national Needs Plan by submitting a governorate-level needs plan to the governorate council, which is then transmitted to MOTS. The distribution committees are responsible for allocating quotas to the districts (*markazes*). The composition of distribution committees varies by governorate but typically representatives from MOTS, consumer cooperatives, the Ministry of Interior, the police, and the local Chamber of Commerce are included. The committees may also include *markaz* officials. However, the program committee in Cairo has the final authority for determining the size of each governorate's quota (Alderman, von Braun, and Sakr 1982).

Regional Allocation of Food Subsidy Benefits

The map of the Arab Republic of Egypt presented in Figure 5.1 locates the governorates. Table 5.1 presents the allocation of food subsidy benefits by governorates in 1997. For each subsidized food, the benefit to consumers has been calculated as the difference between the subsidized price of the food and what households would have to pay for this food in the free market in the absence of food subsidies.[16] This benefit may be interpreted as an income transfer from the government to consumers. The subsidy benefit per unit of commodity is multiplied by the total reported supply of that commodity to each governorate to calculate the total subsidy benefit for that commodity.

Figure 5.2 shows the relationship between the distribution of total food subsidy benefits and population by governorates. Cairo receives preferential treatment in allocation of food subsidy benefits. In Dakhalia, Sharkia, Kafr El-Sheikh, and Behera (all in Lower Egypt), the share of population significantly exceeds the share of benefits. In the remaining 21 governorates, benefits are distributed more or less in accordance with population distribution.

Figure 5.3 and Table 5.2 show the regional differences in 1997 allocations of absolute food subsidy benefits in per capita terms, disaggregated by urban and rural governorates. Clearly, there is a strong urban bias in the allocation of food subsidies in Egypt. At the time of the 1996 census, 57 percent of the Egyptian population lived in rural areas, but only 30 percent of total food subsidies were allocated to rural areas. Recent poverty estimates for Egypt show a higher incidence of poverty in the rural areas than in urban areas (Datt, Jolliffe, and Sharma 1998; Cardiff 1997; INP 1996). A major reason for the difference in the allocation of benefits to urban and rural areas is that much higher quantities of subsidized *baladi* bread are made available to urban dwellers. There are two probable reasons for the urban bias: (1) many rural households are producers of wheat and other staple foods, and therefore they are perceived to depend less on purchased food staples than do their urban counterparts; (2) for political stability, it is important to keep bread prices low for urban consumers.

---

[16] The rates of subsidy vary between subsidized foods. Estimates of "free-market" prices were derived by adding costs of internal transportation, storage, handling, milling, and baking (for bread) to cost, insurance, and freight (c.i.f.) import prices. Thus, the free-market or unsubsidized prices reflect the equivalent international or border prices of the subsidized commodities. These unsubsidized prices are referred to as "full cost" in Table 3.1.

Figure 5.1—Map of the Arab Republic of Egypt

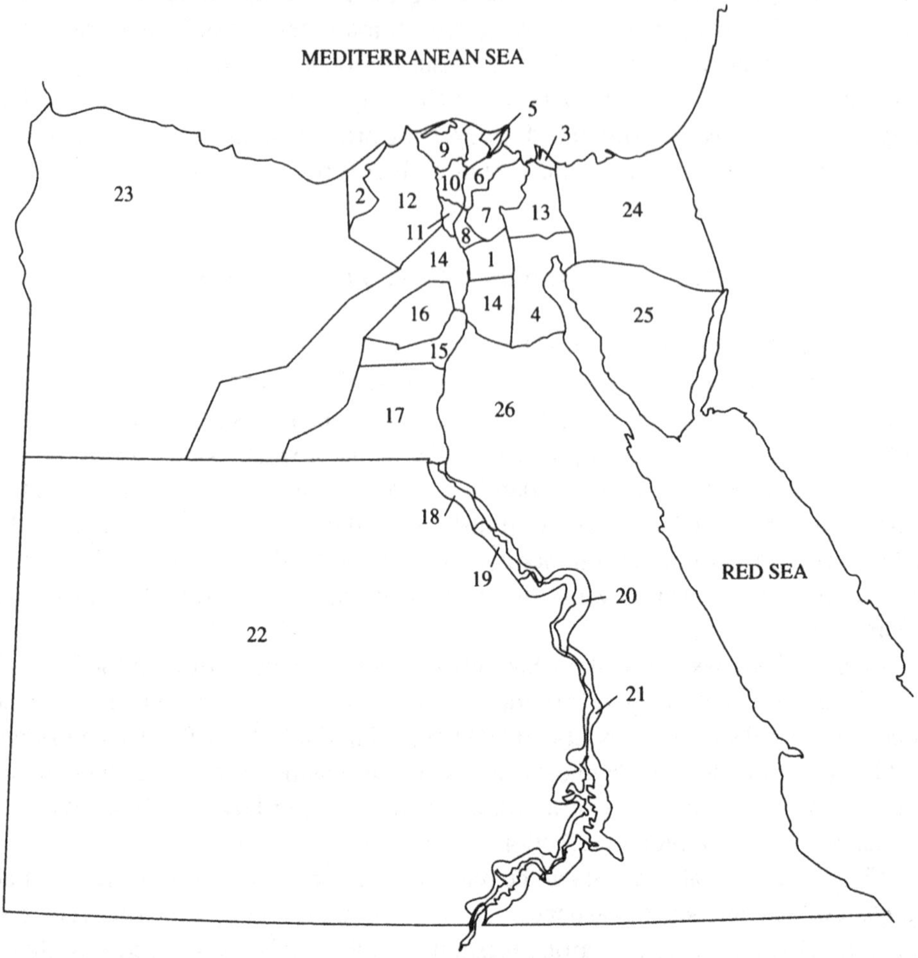

METROPOLITAN GOVERNORATES	LOWER EGYPT	UPPER EGYPT	FRONTIER GOVERNORATES
1 Cairo	5 Damietta	14 Giza	22 New Valley
2 Alexandria	6 Dakahlia	15 Beni-Suef	23 Matrouh
3 Port Said	7 Sharkia	16 Fayoum	24 North Sinai
4 Suez	8 Kalyoubia	17 Menia	25 South Sinai
	9 Kafr El-Sheikh	18 Assyout	26 Red Sea
	10 Gharbia	19 Suhag	
	11 Menoufia	20 Quena	
	12 Behera	21 Aswan	
	13 Ismailia		

Note: The frontier governorates are excluded from this report.

Table 5.1—Allocation of food subsidy benefits, and distribution of population and poverty, by governorates

Governorate	*Baladi* bread	Wheat flour	Sugar	Cooking oil	Total	Population share	INP poverty measure: Head-count poverty (P_0)	INP poverty measure: Contribution to total poverty[b]
	Subsidy benefits, 1997[a]							
	(percent of total benefits)						(percent)	
Cairo	23.9	0.0	15.8	19.2	19.0	11.5	10.8	5.40
Alexandria	8.7	1.0	6.5	9.5	7.3	5.6	29.4	7.21
Port Said	1.1	0.1	0.8	1.2	0.9	0.8	3.7	0.13
Suez	1.0	0.2	0.7	0.7	0.8	0.7	2.4	0.07
Metropolitan	34.8	1.3	23.9	30.5	28.1	18.6	16.0	12.97
Damietta	1.8	3.5	2.0	2.0	2.1	1.5	0.7	0.05
Dakahlia	4.3	0.7	8.0	7.3	4.3	7.1	11.4	3.55
Sharkia	5.3	0.0	5.7	4.0	4.5	7.2	13.9	4.39
Kalyoubia	6.6	0.8	5.2	5.0	5.4	5.6	28.3	6.89
Kafr El-Sheikh	1.2	3.4	4.4	4.4	2.1	3.8	10.1	1.65
Gharbia	4.2	3.7	6.6	5.4	4.5	5.7	9.4	2.36
Menoufia	3.6	7.2	9.9	4.1	4.9	4.7	22.8	4.63
Behera	3.6	5.6	4.4	6.3	4.2	6.7	28.5	8.36
Ismailia	1.6	1.0	1.3	1.5	1.5	1.2	9.7	0.51
Lower Egypt	32.2	25.9	47.5	39.9	33.5	43.5	17.1	32.52
Giza	10.4	6.8	4.8	8.2	9.1	8.1	12.0	4.23
Beni-Suef	2.7	1.2	0.3	0.2	2.0	3.1	34.0	4.66
Fayoum	2.3	7.3	3.7	2.9	3.3	3.4	40.6	5.95
Menia	5.9	0.1	4.3	4.6	4.7	5.6	35.8	8.73
Assyout	3.5	9.1	5.0	2.1	4.5	4.7	53.4	11.02
Suhag	2.7	17.7	0.6	3.0	4.8	5.3	39.4	9.07
Quena	2.5	20.8	5.2	4.7	5.8	4.7	38.3	7.91
Aswan	1.4	7.4	2.9	2.1	2.5	1.6	30.8	2.21
Upper Egypt	31.4	70.3	26.7	27.8	36.7	36.5	34.1	54.36
Frontier governorates	1.6	2.5	1.9	1.8	1.8	1.4	16.0	0.96
Total	100.0	100.0	100.0	100.0	100.0	100.0	22.9	100.0

Sources: Subsidy benefits are calculated by the authors using the 1997 allocations of quantities of subsidized commodities to governorates (see Appendix Tables F.5 and F.6), data obtained from Ministry of Supply and Trade. Population shares are calculated from the 1996 population census data, representing the population living in Egypt (see Appendix Table F.7). Head-count poverty estimates are from the INP (Institute of National Planning), "Egypt Human Development Report 1996," based on the Household Income and Expenditure Survey of 1995/96, conducted by CAPMAS.

[a] For each subsidized food, the benefit to consumers per unit of subsidized food has been calculated as the difference between the subsidized price of the food and what consumers would have to pay for this food in the absence of subsidies (that is, the full costs of the food, provided in Table 3.1). Subsidy benefit per unit of commodity is multiplied by the total reported supply of that commodity to each governorate to calculate the total subsidy benefit for the commodity in that governorate.

[b] Contribution to total poverty is calculated as 100 × (governorate population/total population) × (governorate P_0/total P_0).

Figure 5.2—Distribution of population and food subsidy benefits, by governorates, 1997

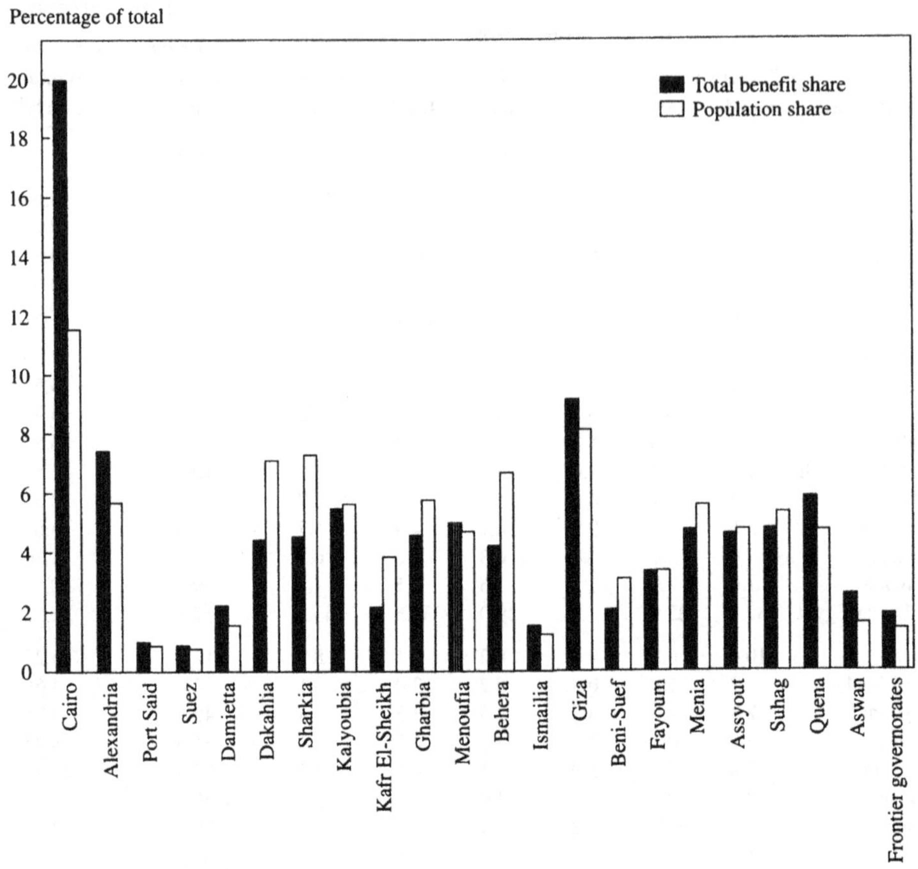

Source: Table 5.1.

If targeting food subsidies to the poor is the goal, then the pattern of allocation of these subsidies should correspond to the geographical distribution of poverty among governorates. How does the current pattern of food subsidy allocation among governorates compare with the pattern of poverty in the current system?

The IFPRI Food Security Research Project in Egypt completed a poverty profile for Egypt based on the 1997 EIHS survey data (Datt, Jolliffe, and Sharma 1998). Reference poverty lines take into account regional differences in food and nonfood prices, age and composition of households, and food and nonfood consumption preferences. Regional reference poverty lines in monthly, per capita figures are as follows: metropolitan, LE 129.19; lower urban, LE 101.72; lower rural, LE 85.38; upper urban, LE 101.36; and upper rural, LE 82.81. The poverty profile provides three types of poverty measurements: the head-count index, or poverty incidence

Figure 5.3—Urban and rural allocation of per capita absolute food subsidy benefits, by governorates, 1997

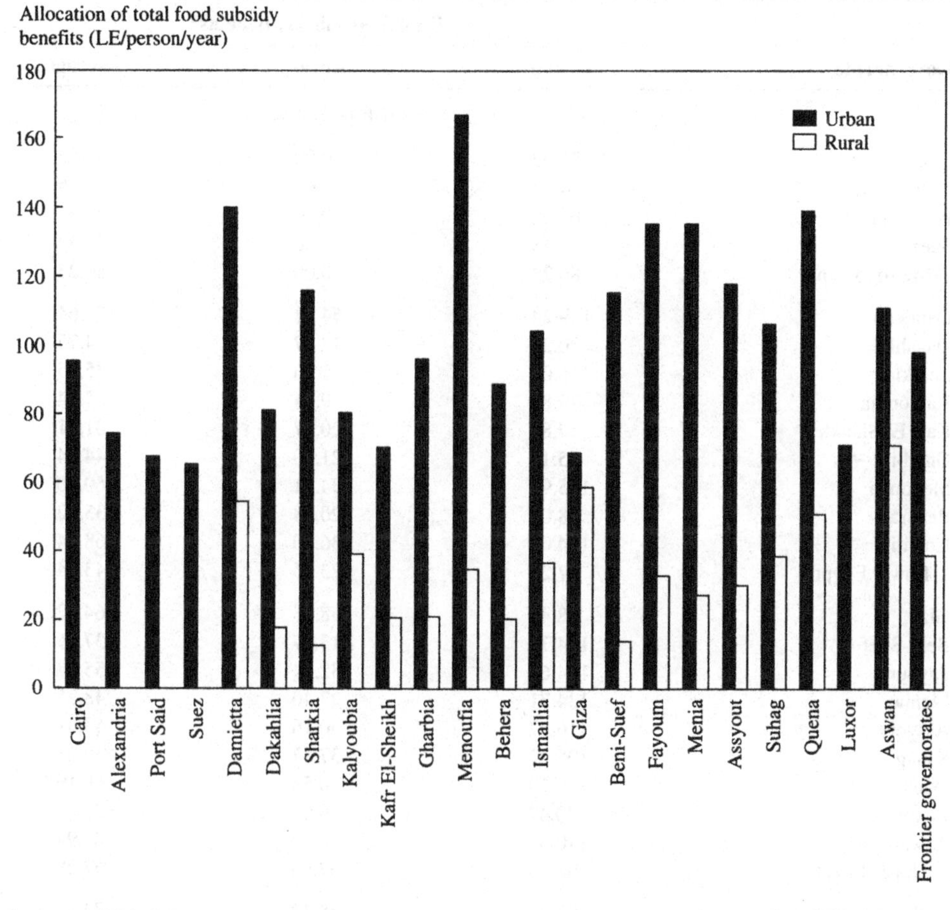

Source: Table 5.2.

(P_0); the poverty gap index, or poverty depth (P_1); and the distribution-sensitive poverty index, or poverty severity (P_2).[17]

Table 5.3 presents the head-count poverty index and the distribution-sensitive poverty index for Egypt and for each of the five regions. The head-count index indicates that 26.5 percent of the population in Egypt was poor in 1997. The poverty

[17] The head-count index (P_0) shows the proportion of the poor population to the total population. The head-count index is a simple poverty measure and its interpretation is straightforward. However, this measure is insensitive to the depth of poverty, which the poverty gap index (P_1) takes into account. The poverty gap is an estimate of the income (or expenditure) that would be required to bring every individual up to the poverty threshold. A reduction in the income of any poor individual would increase the poverty gap (and vice versa), but the poverty head count would remain unchanged. But the poverty gap index is insensitive to the redistribution of income among the poor. As the name indicates, the distribution-sensitive poverty measure (P_2) is sensitive to the reallocation of income among the poor. This poverty measure decreases if income is transferred from a poor individual to a poorer individual (and vice versa).

Table 5.2—Urban and rural allocations of per capita absolute food subsidy benefits, by governorates, 1997

Governorate	Total food subsidy benefits[a] Urban	Rural	Average
		(LE/person/year)	
Cairo	94.62	0.00	94.62
Alexandria	74.36	0.00	74.36
Port Said	67.56	0.00	67.56
Suez	65.43	0.00	65.43
Metropolitan	86.23	0.00	86.23
Damietta	139.24	54.33	77.64
Dakahlia	80.34	17.17	34.75
Sharkia	115.00	11.86	35.15
Kalyoubia	79.88	39.14	55.74
Kafr El-Sheikh	69.83	20.37	31.71
Gharbia	95.19	21.30	44.24
Menoufia	165.93	34.31	60.50
Behera	88.00	20.08	35.62
Ismailia	104.03	36.80	68.84
Lower Egypt	97.23	23.55	43.84
Giza	68.40	58.85	64.02
Beni-Suef	114.72	13.27	37.15
Fayoum	134.60	32.94	55.78
Menia	134.71	27.40	48.25
Assyout	116.97	30.16	53.81
Suhag	105.22	37.37	52.23
Quena	138.59	50.53	69.19
Luxor	70.47	0.00	70.47
Aswan	110.68	70.93	87.94
Upper Egypt	98.93	37.95	57.29
Frontier governorates	97.52	38.49	74.48
Total	92.94	29.99	57.04

Source: Subsidy benefits are calculated by the authors, using the 1997 allocation of quantities of subsidized commodities to governorates, data obtained from the Ministry of Trade and Supply.

[a] For each subsidized food, the benefit to consumers per unit of subsidized food has been calculated as the difference between the subsidized price of the food and what consumers would have to pay for this food in the absence of subsidies (that is, the full cost of the food, provided in Table 3.1). The subsidy benefit per unit of commodity is multiplied by the per capita supply of that commodity to each governorate to calculate the per capita subsidy benefit for the commodity in that governorate.

measure used in this analysis is additively decomposable, making it possible to determine the percentage contribution of any subgroup to total poverty. Table 5.3 provides the percentage share or contribution of each region to the total number living in poverty (P_0) and to the total severity of poverty (P_2). For instance, this analysis suggests that if the poor in the upper rural region were no longer poor, then head-

Table 5.3—Distribution of food subsidy benefits and poverty, by region, 1997

Region	Share of total allocation of food subsidy benefits[a]	Share of total benefits received by consumers	Population share	IFPRI poverty measure: Head-count poverty (P_0)	Distribution sensitive poverty (P_2)	Contribution to total poverty[b] P_0	P_2
	(percent)						
Metropolitan	28.6	22.7	18.8	26.1	2.4	18.5	17.9
Lower urban	20.8	15.5	12.2	24.2	2.0	11.1	9.3
Lower rural	13.3	25.1	31.9	27.0	2.7	32.5	33.2
Upper urban	20.4	13.1	11.7	17.1	1.5	7.5	6.9
Upper rural	16.9	24.1	25.3	31.7	3.3	30.3	32.7
Egypt[c]	100.0	100.0	100.0	26.5	2.6	100.0	100.0

Sources: IFPRI poverty data are from Datt, Jolliffe, and Sharma 1998. Allocation of subsidy benefits are calculated by authors using 1997 data from the Ministry of Trade and Supply for the distribution of subsidized foods (Tables F.5 and F.6). Subsidy benefits received by consumers are calculated from Tables 6.9 to 6.12 in Chapter 6. Population shares are calculated from the 1996 population census data (Table F.7).

[a] For each subsidized food, the benefit to consumers per unit of subsidized food has been calculated as the difference between the subsidized price of the food and what consumers would have to pay for this food in the absence of subsidies (that is, the full cost of the food, provided in Table 3.1). The subsidy benefit per unit of commodity is multiplied by the total reported supply of that commodity to each region to calculate the total subsidy benefit for the commodity in that region.

[b] Contribution to total poverty is calculated as 100 × (region population share) × (region P/total P).

[c] IFPRI poverty measures exclude the frontier governorates. Accordingly, the shares of total food subsidy benefits and population for the frontier governorates are excluded.

count poverty in Egypt as a whole would be reduced by 30.3 percent, while the severity of poverty would be reduced by 32.7 percent.

Figure 5.4 illustrates the shares of food subsidy allocations and poverty by region. At present, the regional allocation of food subsidies is not sensitive to the regional distribution of poverty. Using IFPRI's 1997 regional head-count poverty shares, the urban regions (metropolitan, lower urban, and upper urban) accounted for 37.1 percent of total poverty in Egypt, but they received 69.8 percent of total food subsidy allocations. In contrast, rural areas in Lower and Upper Egypt, which received only 30.2 percent of total subsidy allocations, accounted for 62.8 percent of total poverty.

The IFPRI 1997 poverty profile disaggregates poverty measures by five regions and not by governorates. Governorate-level poverty measures are available from the 1996 Egypt Human Development Report, prepared by the INP. The poverty estimates in the INP study are based on the 1995/96 Household Income and Expenditure Survey, conducted by CAPMAS. The INP's poverty estimate yields a national-level head-count index of 22.9 percent (INP 1996).

Figure 5.4—Food subsidy allocations and distribution of poverty, by region, 1997

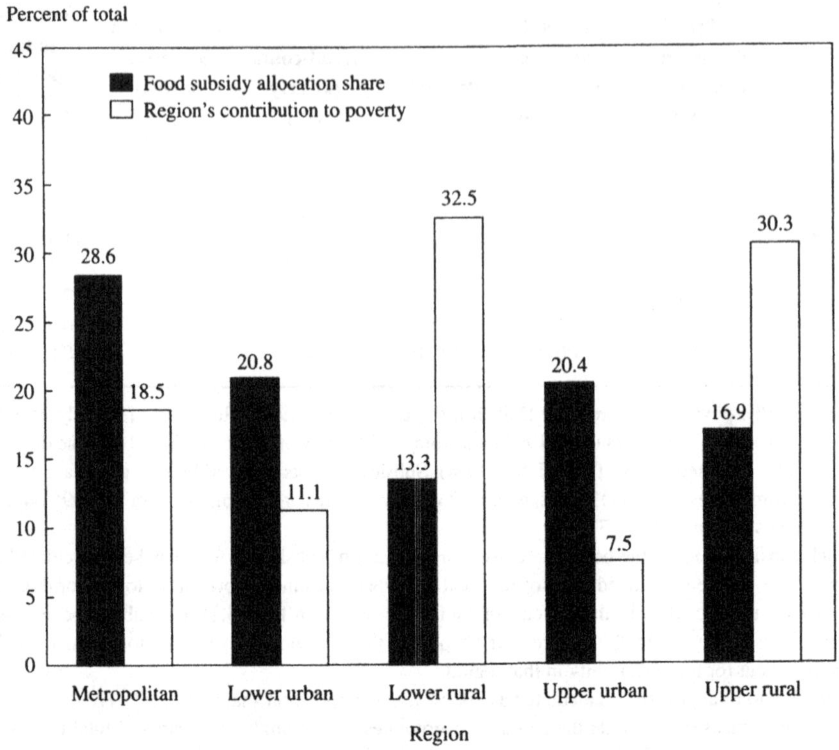

Source: Table 5.3.

Table 5.1 provides the INP head-count poverty index and the contribution of each governorate to total poverty in Egypt. The pattern of distribution of poverty shows a lack of correspondence to the pattern of allocation of food subsidies across governorates. This is consistent with the patterns across regions based on IFPRI's poverty estimates. For instance, Cairo and Giza received 28.1 percent of the total food subsidy benefits in 1996/97, but these two governorates accounted for only 9.6 percent of total poverty in Egypt. In contrast, Assyout, Behera, Beni-Suef, Fayoum, Menia, Quena, and Suhag, which accounted for 55.7 percent of total poverty, received only 29.3 percent of total food subsidies.

The regional pattern of allocation of food subsidies is, however, quite different from the regional pattern of distribution of food subsidy benefits actually received by consumers. Table 5.3 shows that the shares of total food subsidy benefits received by consumers in the five regions correspond closely to the regional population shares and the regional distribution of total poverty.[18] Why is the supply-

[18] Chapter 6 provides estimates of food subsidy benefits received by consumers.

side pattern different from the demand-side pattern? This difference can mainly be attributed to two factors: (1) benefits received by consumers are net of system leakages of subsidized foods,[19] and the magnitude of these leakages vary widely among the regions; (2) bakeries producing subsidized *baladi* bread are highly concentrated in urban areas, and, therefore, the allocation of subsidized flour to urban bakeries is much greater. On average, urban areas have about 30 bakeries per 100,000 urban population, while rural areas have only 9 bakeries per 100,000 rural population. However, many rural residents purchase subsidized *baladi* bread from outlets located in their neighboring urban centers. Therefore, the purchased quantity of subsidized *baladi* bread by rural consumers is higher than the allocation of flour to rural bakeries for subsidized *baladi* bread production. As a result, the subsidy benefits received by rural consumers are higher than the allocation indicates.[20] While this practice helps mitigate some of the urban bias in the allocation of food subsidies, the rural consumers nevertheless accrue transaction costs (for travel, for example), which reduces their real benefits to the extent that such transactions occur.

This analysis suggests a role for improved geographical targeting of food subsidies at the governorate level as a means to bring greater benefits to the poor. In order to increase the accuracy of geographic targeting of food subsidies in Egypt, a two-step method could be followed. First, the total annual food subsidy resources could be allocated to each governorate according to its contribution to total poverty. Second, at the governorate level, a larger share of total food subsidies received could be distributed in villages and urban neighborhoods where the poor are known to be concentrated. Political considerations such as favoritism toward the politically more influential urban consumers, of course, may prevent such allocations (in the bargaining and negotiation between governorate-level distribution committees and the national-level program committee), based simply on where the poor live.

Nevertheless, geographic targeting can be highly cost-effective. For example, a Philippine study demonstrates that a geographically targeted program costing 2 billion pesos can reduce poverty by as much as a general food subsidy costing 18 billion pesos (Balisacan 1994). Experience in the Philippines with a pilot food subsidy scheme suggests that targeting by location is logistically simple and, thus, represents a low-cost form of targeting food subsidies (Garcia and Pinstrup-Andersen 1987). Many social programs in Latin America use geographic targeting. Simulations using household survey data from Jamaica, Mexico, and Venezuela show that both leakage to the nonpoor and undercoverage of the poor diminish as the size of the targeted geographic area gets smaller (Grosh 1994).

---

[19] Leakage is defined as the illegal diversion of subsidized foods for sale at higher prices in black markets or open markets, before subsidized foods reach the consumers. Chapter 6 presents estimates of leakage.

[20] *Baladi* bread is by far the most important subsidized food in Egypt, accounting for 61.7 percent of total food subsidies in 1996/97.

Household-Level Use of the Food Subsidy System

This section addresses household use of food subsidies in Lower and Upper Egypt, by urban and rural areas, and by income group. The discussion is based on data collected in the 1997 EIHS, described in Chapter 4.[21]

Baladi *Bread and Wheat Flour*

Table 5.4 shows regional differences in per capita purchases of subsidized and open-market bread and flour. Subsidized *baladi* bread is purchased at a higher rate in urban areas and subsidized *baladi* wheat flour is purchased at a higher rate in rural areas. Because *baladi* bread enjoys a higher rate of subsidy than does wheat flour, the different purchasing patterns probably reflect differences largely in access (supply) rather than choice (demand).[22] Bakeries are more highly concentrated in urban areas. On average, urban areas have about 30 bakeries per 100,000 population, while rural areas have only 9 bakeries per 100,000 population (see Appendix F, Table F.4).

Figure 5.5 shows the average share of households in each expenditure quintile that purchased subsidized *baladi* bread and wheat flour at the national level at the time of the survey. As indicated in Table 5.5, a very high percentage of households living in metropolitan governorates purchased subsidized *baladi* bread (92.5 percent). This percentage was somewhat higher for the lowest quintile than for the highest quintile. Despite the low concentration of bakeries in rural areas, and the fact that allocation of subsidized wheat flour to rural bakeries is only about one-sixth of the urban quota, 56.1 percent of the rural households reported purchases of subsidized *baladi* bread during the week prior to the date of interview.

Purchases of *baladi* wheat flour were much lower at all levels. At the national level, 19 percent of all Egyptian households purchased subsidized wheat flour. About 30 percent of households in rural areas purchased subsidized wheat flour. Metropolitan governorates are not offered subsidized wheat flour. In the governorates outside of the metropolitan region, only 13 percent of urban households purchased subsidized wheat flour. Both subsidized and open-market purchases of wheat flour are

---

[21] Much of the household-level analysis in this report disaggregates the population of the sample households into quintile groups. Quintile groups are based on population quintiles ranked by total per capita expenditures. A "fitted" total expenditure per capita variable was calculated for each household. From this point on, "expenditure quintile" should be understood to mean population in any stratum (such as metropolitan, urban, rural, upper, lower) ranked using fitted total expenditure per capita.

Although income data are available in the EIHS, per capita expenditures are used as a proxy for income for two reasons. First, expenditures are likely to reflect permanent income and are, hence, a better indicator of consumption behavior. Second, data on expenditures are generally more reliable and stable than income data. Because expenditures are intended to proxy for income, the terms "expenditure" and "income" will be used interchangeably.

[22] The purchase figures for subsidized wheat flour, when aggregated over all households, are consistent with government figures on the supply of *baladi* wheat flour distributed to urban and rural areas. However, figures for *baladi* bread purchases in rural areas are considerably higher than the aggregate national-level distribution of subsidized wheat flour to rural bakeries. This difference is probably because many rural households purchase subsidized *baladi* bread from neighboring urban outlets.

Table 5.4—Per capita purchases of subsidized and open-market bread and flour, by region

Commodities	Metropolitan	Lower urban	Lower rural	Upper urban	Upper rural	Egypt[a]
Subsidized *baladi* bread (loaves/day)	2.6	2.8	1.4	2.2	1.4	1.9
White *baladi* bread (loaves/day)	0.1	n.a.	0.1	0.1	n.a.	0.1
Shami bread (loaves/day)	n.a.	n.a.	n.a.	n.a.	n.a.	n.a.
Fino bread (loaves/day)	0.6	0.3	0.1	0.6	0.1	0.3
Subsidized wheat flour (kilograms/month)	0.0	0.3	1.0	1.4	3.7	1.2
Open-market wheat flour (kilograms/month)	0.3	0.6	0.8	0.6	2.3	1.0
Maize flour (kilograms/month)	0.1	0.4	2.1	0.5	2.2	1.4

Source: IFPRI Food Security Research Project in Egypt, "Egypt Integrated Household Survey, 1997."
Note: n.a. = negligible amount.
[a] Data for Egypt are weighted averages by regional population.

much higher in rural Upper Egypt than in rural Lower Egypt. Consumption of own-produced wheat and rice is higher in rural Lower Egypt.

Table 5.6 provides estimates of absolute benefits (or income transfers) to consumers from subsidized *baladi* bread and wheat flour, by region and expenditure quintile. The absolute food subsidy benefit to a household, or income transfer, is the difference between what households actually pay for subsidized foods and what they would have paid for these foods in the free market in the absence of food subsidies. Estimates of "free-market" prices were derived by adding costs of internal transport, storage, handling, milling, and baking to cost, insurance, and freight (c.i.f.) import prices of wheat. Thus, the free-market or unsubsidized prices reflect the equivalent international or border prices of the subsidized commodities. Subsidized *baladi* bread and wheat flour prices were estimated to be 57 percent and 43 percent below free-market prices, respectively.[23]

The average per capita monthly benefits from subsidized *baladi* bread were higher in metropolitan (LE 5.22) and other urban areas (LE 4.95) than in rural areas (LE 2.78). Benefits declined with income in metropolitan areas, but did not vary markedly with income for other urban and rural households (Table 5.6). The average national-level benefit from subsidized wheat flour was relatively small, only LE 0.56 per capita per month, although benefits were relatively higher for rural households. As Table 5.6 shows, benefits were somewhat higher for middle-income groups. Fig-

[23] In Chapter 3, it was reported that the government sold subsidized *baladi* wheat flour *to bakers* at 70 percent below full cost. Because consumers pay for the cost of baking the bread, the subsidy to consumers is a lower percentage.

Figure 5.5—Share of households purchasing subsidized *baladi* bread and wheat flour, all Egypt by expenditure quintile, 1997

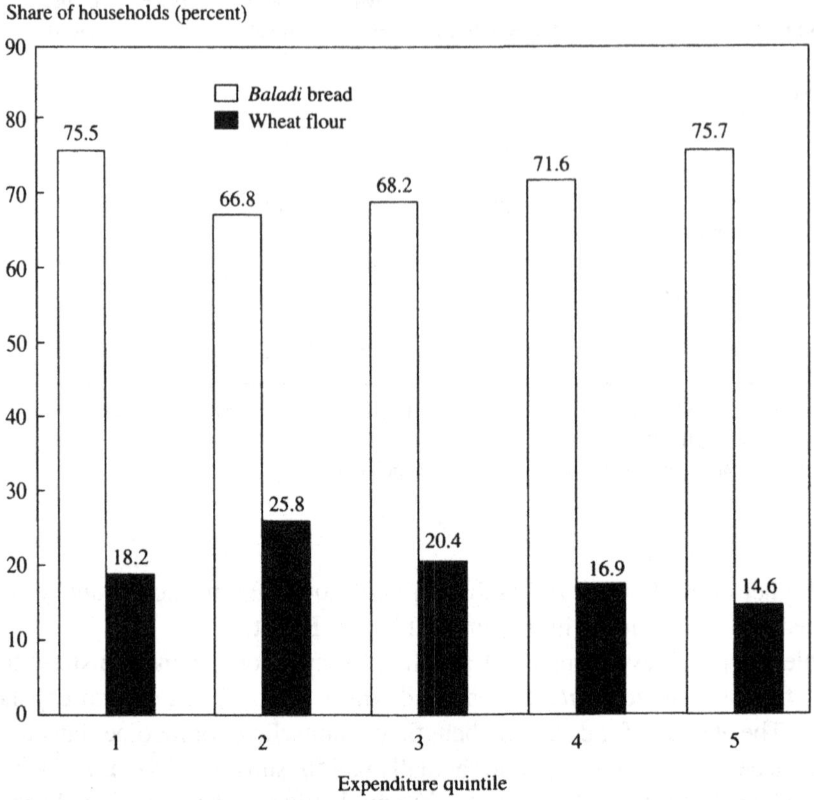

Source: Table 5.5.
Note: One is the lowest quintile and five is the highest.

ure 5.6 illustrates the pattern of distribution of absolute benefits from subsidized *baladi* bread and wheat flour among expenditure quintiles at the national level.

With respect to the income transfers derived from consumption of *baladi* bread, some Egyptians are concerned that, because the rate of subsidy is so high (and the bread is therefore so inexpensive), much of it is wasted, particularly if it is fed to animals. Indeed, there is a perception that the percentage of subsidized bread diverted to feed poultry and sometimes larger animals is high (Sadowski 1991). The household survey results indicate that 13.0 percent of all households purchasing *baladi* bread fed some or all of it to animals. Of those households who fed *baladi* bread to animals, 7.2 percent of their total purchased bread was fed to animals. Thus, only about 1 percent of all *baladi* bread purchased was fed to animals.[24]

[24] The figures reported by households on *baladi* bread fed to animals may understate this use of bread in that households might perceive this as an immoral act; therefore, they may have reported a lower than actual amount to survey enumerators.

Table 5.5—Share of households purchasing subsidized *baladi* bread and wheat flour, by region and expenditure quintile

Commodity Region	Lowest (1)	(2)	(3)	(4)	Highest (5)	Average
	Per capita expenditure quintile					
	(percent of all survey households)					
Baladi bread						
Egypt	75.5	66.8	68.2	71.6	75.7	71.7
Metropolitan	98.6	94.8	86.0	93.7	89.6	92.5
Other urban	91.4	84.4	83.8	80.1	82.4	83.7
Rural	58.2	51.5	57.1	55.4	59.5	56.1
Wheat flour						
Egypt	18.2	25.8	20.4	16.9	14.6	19.0
Metropolitan	0.0	0.0	0.0	0.0	0.0	0.0
Other urban	14.0	13.8	15.8	12.0	11.3	13.0
Rural	28.1	38.3	27.8	28.4	28.0	30.4

Source: IFPRI Food Security Research Project in Egypt, "Egypt Integrated Household Survey, 1997."

Outlet characteristics influence the extent to which households purchase subsidized foods and these characteristics may affect poor and rich households differently. For example, food subsidies can effectively target the poor (indirectly without resorting to a means test) if subsidized food distribution outlets are concentrated in poor neighborhoods. Table 5.7 shows, however, that there is little difference between income groups in the average traveling time from household to *baladi* bread outlet. In fact, in all regions, the average distance from a household to an outlet (in terms of minutes of walking) is slightly longer for the poorest 20 percent of the population than for the richest 20 percent. Because poorer neighborhoods are expected to be more densely populated than richer neighborhoods, this suggests that the concentration of outlets relative to numbers of people served is higher in richer than in poorer neighborhoods.

Related to travel time is the cost of waiting time. As shown in Table 5.8, it takes approximately half an hour waiting time to purchase subsidized *baladi* bread in the metropolitan and other urban areas, with longer waiting times in rural areas. In all regions, waiting times of higher-income consumers are shorter than those of lower-income consumers.[25]

After travel and waiting time is incurred, any quantity of subsidized *baladi* bread and wheat flour are available to consumers, in theory, without restrictions. Only 14 percent of the households surveyed reported limitations on the quantity of *baladi* bread purchased per transaction. However, the prevalence of per transaction limita-

[25] It could be argued that high-income consumers simply avoid purchasing *baladi* bread when lines and waiting times are long (waiting time is an endogenous decision rather than an outlet characteristic). Note, however, that there are not large differences between poor and rich households in their purchases of *baladi* bread.

Table 5.6—Per capita monthly absolute benefits to consumers from subsidized *baladi* bread and wheat flour, by region and expenditure quintile

	Per capita expenditure quintile					
Commodity Region	Lowest (1)	(2)	(3)	(4)	Highest (5)	Average
	(LE/person/month)					
Baladi bread						
Egypt	4.14	3.58	3.92	3.84	4.08	3.91
Metropolitan	6.23	6.05	4.95	5.02	4.40	5.22
Other urban	5.50	4.98	5.24	4.93	4.54	4.95
Rural	2.62	2.30	3.10	2.55	3.41	2.78
Wheat flour						
Egypt	0.41	0.70	0.62	0.60	0.45	0.56
Metropolitan	0.00	0.00	0.00	0.00	0.00	0.00
Other urban	0.30	0.33	0.52	0.35	0.30	0.35
Rural	0.65	1.05	0.83	1.07	0.92	0.91

Source: IFPRI Food Security Research Project in Egypt, "Egypt Integrated Household Survey, 1997."

tions on subsidized flour rationing was much higher—46 percent of urban households[26] and 43 percent of rural households that purchased subsidized flour reported that subsidized flour was available only in limited quantities (Table 5.9).

The Ration System

The ration subsidies on sugar and cooking oil are available on a monthly per capita quota basis to those who hold ration cards.[27] Table 5.10 shows that most Egyptian families (82.9 percent) hold ration cards: 72.3 percent of the households reported that they held green ration cards, 10.6 percent held red ration cards, and 17.1 percent did not possess a ration card.[28] Green ration cards entitle holders to a higher rate of subsidy than do red ration cards (see Table 3.1 for the rates of subsidy). Figure 5.7 shows the percentage of households holding green, red, and no cards by expenditure quintile. The share of households without ration cards is highest in the highest expenditure quintile (27.2 percent) and lowest in the lowest expenditure quintile

---

[26] Subsidized wheat flour is not supplied to the metropolitan governorates (Cairo, Alexandria, Port Said, and Suez). Other urban centers receive subsidized wheat flour.

[27] Enumerators involved in the EIHS were instructed to ask respondents to show their ration cards during interviews.

[28] Coverage of the *population* in the ration card system was 69.2 percent in 1996/97 (see Chapter 3 under the heading Subsidized Sugar and Cooking Oil). The 1997 EIHS results indicate that 82.9 percent of Egyptian *households* held ration cards. The main reason why the share of population coverage is less than the share of household coverage is that the number of registered members (beneficiaries) with household ration cards is less than the total number of household members, primarily because the Ministry of Trade and Supply discontinued registering newborn children into the ration system in 1989.

Figure 5.6—Per capita monthly absolute benefits to consumers from subsidized *baladi* bread and wheat flour, all Egypt by expenditure quintile

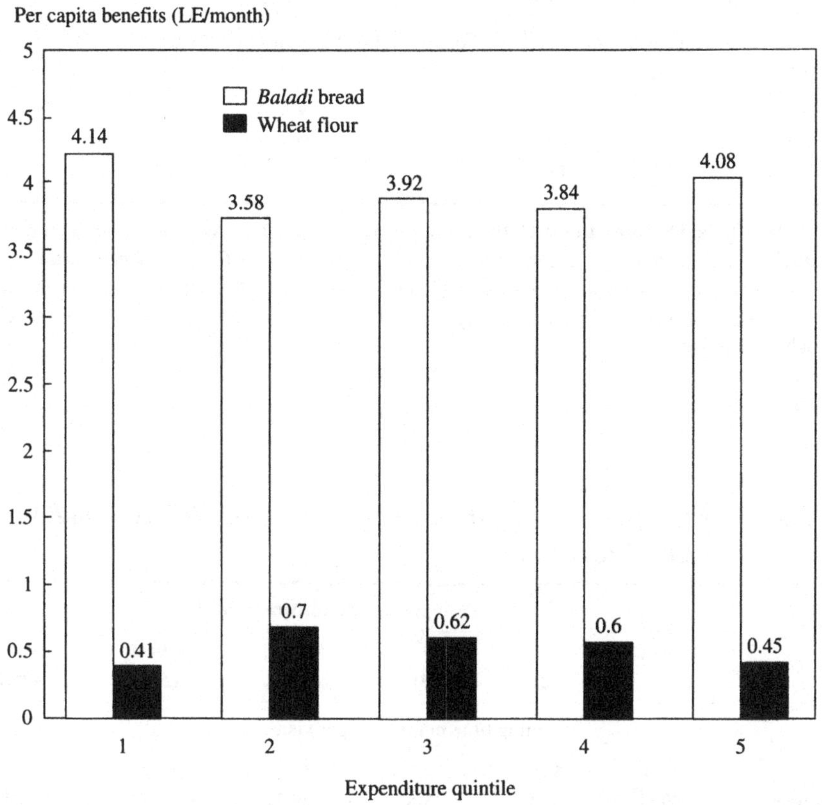

Source: Table 5.6.
Note: One is the lowest quintile and five is the highest.

(11.0 percent). The share of households holding ration cards is higher in rural than in urban areas.

These data highlight ways in which the ration card system is poorly targeted. First, while it is generally assumed that the households without ration cards are the richer households, 11 out of every 100 households in the poorest quintile and 16 out of every 100 households in the second poorest quintile do not hold ration cards. Second, 11 percent of households in the poorest quintile and 9 percent of households in the richest quintile hold red cards, which are in principle intended for people in higher-income jobs. Red ration cards are distributed more or less evenly across all income groups (Table 5.11). In fact, 61 percent of households that hold green ration cards, intended for the poor, belong to the three richest expenditure quintiles.

A family's ability to purchase subsidized sugar and cooking oil on the ration card system is also influenced by how many members of the household are registered on

Table 5.7—Average travel time to *baladi* bread outlets, by expenditure quintile

Region	Per capita expenditure quintile					
	Lowest (1)	(2)	(3)	(4)	Highest (5)	Average
	(travel time from household to outlet in minutes of walking)					
Egypt	11.2	9.9	10.3	10.1	9.6	10.2
Metropolitan	9.6	8.0	7.3	8.5	8.1	8.4
Other urban	10.7	9.4	10.9	9.4	9.4	9.8
Rural[a]	13.0	11.8	11.5	12.3	11.6	12.0

Source: IFPRI Food Security Research Project in Egypt, "Egypt Integrated Household Survey, 1997."

[a] Many rural residents commute to neighboring urban centers by vehicles for employment or trade and purchase subsidized *baladi* bread from outlets located in urban areas. Since their commuting time is not primarily spent for purchasing *baladi* bread, the average travel time reported for rural residents in this table excludes such commuting time.

Table 5.8—Average time waiting in line to purchase subsidized *baladi* bread, by expenditure quintile

Region	Per capita expenditure quintile					
	Lowest (1)	(2)	(3)	(4)	Highest (5)	Average
	(waiting time in minutes per visit)					
Egypt	35.0	34.3	32.3	30.2	25.8	31.1
Metropolitan	29.6	31.8	25.5	28.5	25.0	27.9
Other urban	33.9	33.4	27.1	25.9	23.5	27.8
Rural	39.9	36.3	38.2	35.6	29.7	36.1

Source: IFPRI Food Security Research Project in Egypt, "Egypt Integrated Household Survey, 1997."

Table 5.9—Restrictions on subsidized *baladi* bread and wheat flour purchases, by expenditure quintile

Commodities	Metropolitan	Other urban	Rural	Egypt
	(percent of households reporting limits on purchase)			
Baladi bread	10.8	17.1	13.2	13.7
Wheat flour	. . .	46.1	43.1	44.0

Source: IFPRI Food Security Research Project in Egypt, "Egypt Integrated Household Survey, 1997."

Note: Ellipsis (. . .) indicates not applicable.

Table 5.10—Share of households holding ration cards, by expenditure quintile

Region/ Type of card	Lowest (1)	(2)	(3)	(4)	Highest (5)	Average
	Per capita expenditure quintile					
	(percent of all survey households)					
Egypt						
Green card	78.0	74.3	78.0	70.8	63.5	72.3
Red card	11.0	9.5	10.8	12.4	9.3	10.6
No card	11.0	16.2	11.2	16.8	27.2	17.1
Total	100.0	100.0	100.0	100.0	100.0	100.0
Metropolitan						
Green card	78.3	75.9	68.0	59.5	59.4	66.9
Red card	10.1	8.6	20.0	16.5	6.6	11.6
No card	11.6	15.5	12.0	24.0	34.0	21.5
Total	100.0	100.0	100.0	100.0	100.0	100.0
Other urban						
Green card	75.1	66.3	69.7	69.5	59.4	66.8
Red card	15.2	14.2	15.6	12.9	9.1	12.7
No card	9.7	19.5	14.7	17.6	31.5	20.5
Total	100.0	100.0	100.0	100.0	100.0	100.0
Rural						
Green card	79.1	76.9	84.1	77.2	70.3	77.8
Red card	9.6	8.0	6.4	10.1	11.4	9.0
No card	11.3	15.1	9.5	12.7	18.3	13.2
Total	100.0	100.0	100.0	100.0	100.0	100.0

Source: IFPRI Food Security Research Project in Egypt, "Egypt Integrated Household Survey, 1997."
Note: The green ration cards provide a higher rate of subsidy to consumers than do the red ration cards. See Table 3.1 for the rates of subsidy.

the ration card, since each registered member has a ration quota. Table 5.12 indicates that, at the national level, 57.7 percent of the ration card-holding households had one or more household members who were not registered. The prevalence of households with unregistered members is higher in rural areas than in metropolitan and other urban areas, and the incidence of ration card-holding households with unregistered members is markedly higher for low-income households relative to high-income households. On average, about 28 percent of household members in the poorest quintile are not registered, compared with only about 10 percent for households in the richest quintile (Figure 5.8 and Table 5.12). When asked why some members were excluded, a higher proportion of the poorest households reported that they were not allowed to register all household members (Table 5.13).

Table 5.12 also shows the average household size of the card-holding households and the number of household members registered for ration cards by expenditure quintile for Egypt as a whole and by region. Poorer households are much larger. The average household size declines from 7.8 for the poorest quintile to 4.9 for the richest quintile. Poor households also tend to be larger in rural areas than in urban

Figure 5.7—Share of households holding ration cards, all Egypt by expenditure quintile

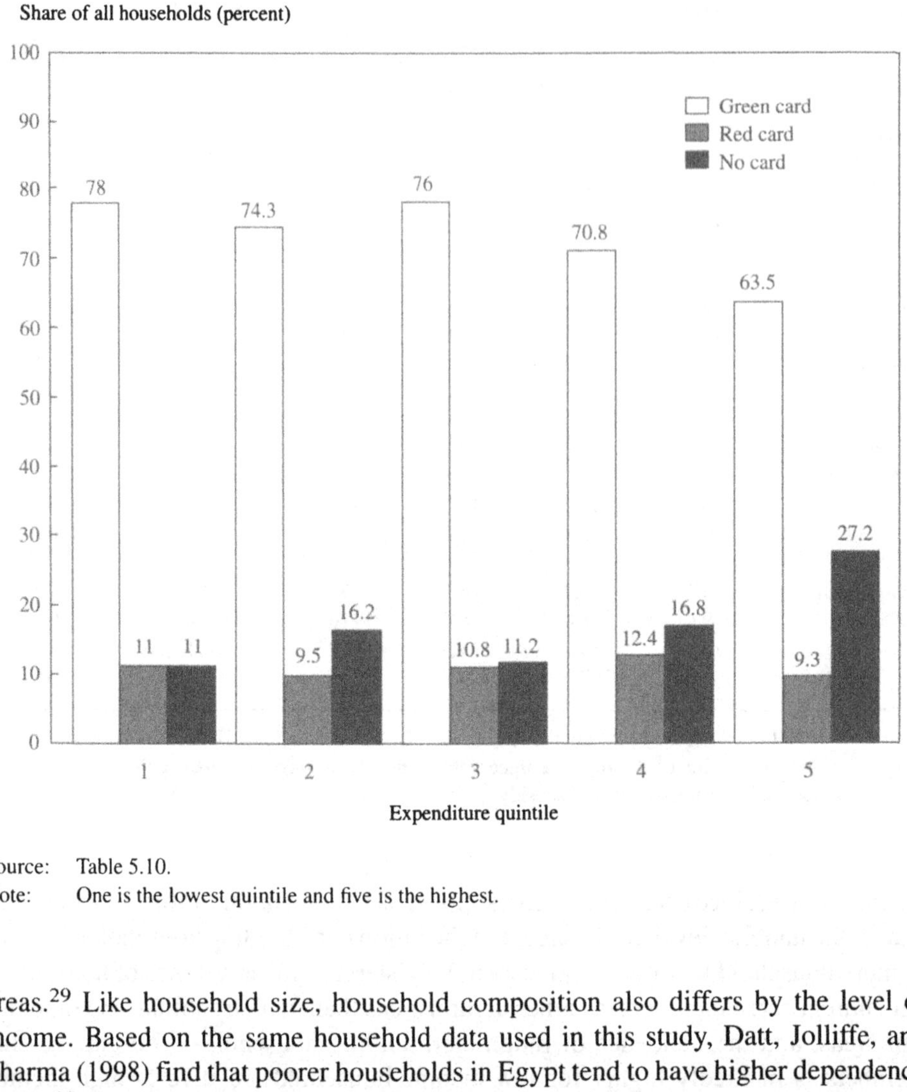

Source: Table 5.10.
Note: One is the lowest quintile and five is the highest.

areas.[29] Like household size, household composition also differs by the level of income. Based on the same household data used in this study, Datt, Jolliffe, and Sharma (1998) find that poorer households in Egypt tend to have higher dependency ratios.[30] The dependency ratio is 127 percent for the ultra poor, 101 percent for the poor (including the ultra poor), and 74 percent for the nonpoor.[31] The difference between the poor and the nonpoor households' total dependency ratios is almost entirely the result of the difference in the number of children present rather than the

[29] This pattern—that poorer households tend to be larger and to have more children—is consistent with other evidence for Egypt and for other developing countries (Datt, Jolliffe, and Sharma 1998).

[30] The dependency ratio is defined as the ratio of the number of household members in the age groups 0–15 years and above 60 years to the number of members of working age 15–60 years.

[31] This pattern is similar for urban and rural areas.

Table 5.11—Households with green and red ration cards, by expenditure quintile

Region/ Type of card	Per capita expenditure quintile Lowest (1)	(2)	(3)	(4)	Highest (5)	Average
	(percent of ration card-holding households)					
Egypt						
Green card	18.8	19.8	20.0	20.4	21.0	100.0
Red card	18.3	17.4	18.9	24.5	20.9	100.0
Metropolitan						
Green card	22.3	18.2	14.0	19.5	26.0	100.0
Red card	16.7	11.9	23.7	31.0	16.7	100.0
Other urban						
Green card	16.6	15.7	16.8	23.8	27.1	100.0
Red card	17.6	17.6	19.7	23.3	21.8	100.0
Rural						
Green card	18.8	22.3	23.7	19.1	16.1	100.0
Red card	19.7	20.1	15.6	21.9	22.7	100.0

Source: IFPRI Food Security Research Project in Egypt, "Egypt Integrated Household Survey, 1997."
Note: The green ration cards provide a higher rate of subsidy to consumers than do the red ration cards. See Table 3.1 for the rates of subsidy.

number of aged. On average, compared with the nonpoor, poor households have one extra child to support for every four adult members of working age.

In 1989, in an effort to reduce the costs of rationed subsidies, MOTS stopped registering newborn children for the ration system. The enforcement of this regulation, as well as the demographic differences just discussed, explain why poorer households have a larger percentage of unregistered household members. Thus, the regulation prohibiting registration of newborns hurts poor households much more than rich households.

With this as background, Table 5.14 shows regional differences in per capita purchases of subsidized (rationed) and open-market sugar and cooking oil. At the national level, per capita sugar purchases amount to 2.27 kilograms per month, of which about 30 percent is obtained from the ration system. There is little variation by region in the quantities purchased from the ration system, but open-market purchases are higher in Upper Egypt.

Both subsidized and open-market purchases of cooking oil are somewhat higher in urban areas than in rural areas. The total per capita quantity of cooking oil purchased per month from both sources is about double (1.09 kilograms) in the metropolitan region than in the upper rural region (0.49 kilograms). Overall, rationed cooking oil accounts for about one-third of total oil purchases in Egypt.

If the quantity of the ration is less than the quantity of that commodity a consumer would have purchased from the open market in the absence of the ration, then the

Table 5.12—Prevalence of unregistered members in the ration card-holding households, by expenditure quintile

	Per capita expenditure quintile					
Region/Item	**Lowest (1)**	**(2)**	**(3)**	**(4)**	**Highest (5)**	**Average**
Households reporting unregistered members	(percent of all ration card-holding households)					
Egypt	72.9	59.1	63.3	51.7	46.2	57.7
Metropolitan	63.8	56.9	56.0	41.8	42.5	50.6
Other urban	66.3	46.3	54.0	48.6	39.7	49.0
Rural	79.8	64.7	69.0	58.6	54.9	65.5
Household size, registered persons, and share of unregistered members	(average number of persons per ration card-holding household)					
Egypt						
Household size	7.8	6.4	6.0	5.3	4.9	6.0
Registered persons	5.6	5.1	4.8	4.5	4.4	4.9
Unregistered members (percent)	28.2	20.3	20.0	15.1	10.2	18.3
Metropolitan						
Household size	5.8	5.3	5.4	4.6	4.4	5.0
Registered persons	5.0	5.1	4.8	4.3	4.2	4.6
Unregistered members (percent)	13.8	3.8	13.0	6.5	4.5	8.0
Other urban						
Household size	7.0	5.4	5.7	4.5	4.3	5.2
Registered persons	5.3	4.6	4.8	4.1	3.9	4.5
Unregistered members (percent)	24.3	14.8	15.8	8.9	9.3	13.5
Rural						
Household size	9.1	7.1	6.3	6.1	5.6	6.8
Registered persons	6.1	5.3	4.8	4.8	4.8	5.2
Unregistered members (percent)	33.0	25.4	23.8	21.3	14.3	23.5

Source: IFPRI Food Security Research Project in Egypt, "Egypt Integrated Household Survey, 1997."

ration is termed "*inframarginal.*" In this case, any change in the price of an inframarginal subsidized ration commodity will have only an income effect to the household and no price (that is, substitution) effect. This implies that the marginal price at which a household determines its budget allocation is the open-market price, not the ration price. The purchase data in Table 5.14 suggest that rationed sugar and cooking oil are inframarginal for Egyptian consumers. Therefore, in theory, any change in ration prices of subsidized sugar and oil would not affect household budget allocation except through a (relatively small) income effect.

Figure 5.8—Share of household members not registered on the ration cards, all Egypt by expenditure quintile

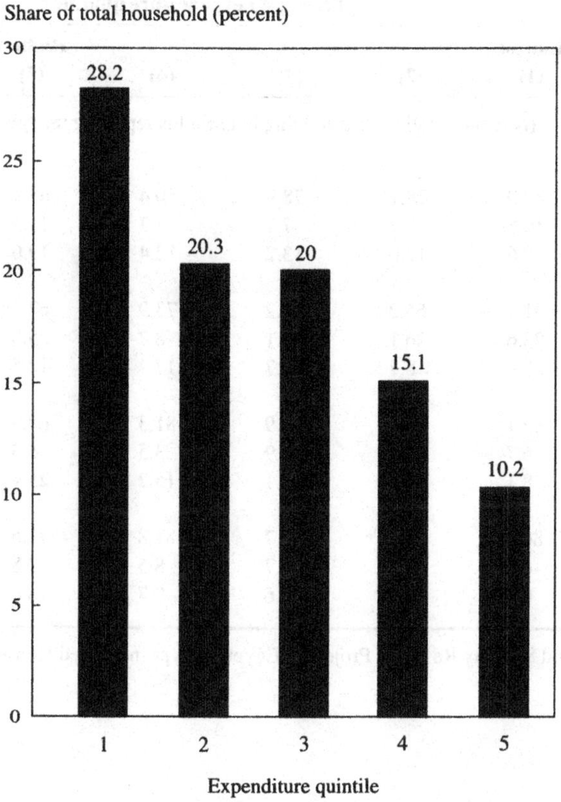

Source: Table 5.12.
Note: One is the lowest quintile and five is the highest.

Table 5.15 indicates that the majority of Egyptians in all income groups and in all regions purchase rationed sugar and cooking oil at subsidized prices. Overall, about three-fourths of all households reported that they had purchased rationed sugar and cooking oil during the previous month. Figure 5.9 shows that the percentage of households that purchase rationed sugar and oil declines somewhat as income increases.

Table 5.16 provides estimates of income transfers to consumers from subsidized sugar and cooking oil, by region and expenditure quintile. For both sugar and oil, the absolute amount of benefits received is more or less similar across income groups (Figure 5.10). On average at the national level, benefits from the sugar subsidy are double those of subsidized oil. The ration benefits are, however, very small. On the average, subsidy benefits from sugar and oil amount to only about LE 1.00 per capita per month.

Table 5.13—Self-reported reasons for unregistered household members, by expenditure quintile

Region/Reasons	Per capita expenditure quintile Lowest (1)	(2)	(3)	(4)	Highest (5)	Average
	(percent of ration card-holding households reporting unregistered members)					
Egypt						
Not allowed	80.0	78.1	78.9	80.4	68.9	77.6
Did not try	10.5	8.9	7.9	7.3	11.5	9.2
Other	9.6	13.0	13.2	12.4	19.6	13.2
Metropolitan						
Not allowed	51.4	65.2	72.2	73.9	62.5	63.4
Did not try	28.6	26.1	11.1	8.7	25.0	21.1
Other	20.0	8.7	16.7	17.4	12.5	15.4
Other urban						
Not allowed	85.1	83.6	76.9	81.3	68.3	78.7
Did not try	6.7	0.0	6.9	3.5	6.3	5.0
Other	8.1	16.4	16.1	15.2	25.4	16.3
Rural						
Not allowed	86.9	79.4	80.7	81.8	71.6	80.9
Did not try	6.2	7.5	7.7	8.5	9.8	7.7
Other	6.9	13.1	11.6	9.7	18.6	11.4

Source: IFPRI Food Security Research Project in Egypt, "Egypt Integrated Household Survey, 1997."

Table 5.14—Per capita purchases of rationed and open-market sugar and cooking oil by region

Commodity	Metropolitan	Lower urban	Lower rural	Upper urban	Upper rural	Egypt
	(purchases in kilograms/person/month)					
Rationed sugar purchase	0.71	0.65	0.68	0.68	0.64	0.67
Open-market sugar purchase	1.20	1.40	1.40	1.90	2.10	1.60
Share of rationed sugar in total sugar purchase (percent)	37.2	31.7	32.7	26.4	23.4	30.3
Rationed cooking oil purchase	0.35	0.23	0.21	0.28	0.20	0.25
Open-market cooking oil purchase	0.74	0.61	0.48	0.54	0.29	0.50
Share of rationed oil in total oil purchase (percent)	32.1	27.4	30.4	34.1	40.8	33.3

Source: IFPRI Food Security Research Project in Egypt, "Egypt Integrated Household Survey, 1997."

Table 5.15—Share of all households purchasing subsidized sugar and cooking oil, by region and expenditure quintile

	Per capita expenditure quintile					
Commodity/Region	**Lowest (1)**	**(2)**	**(3)**	**(4)**	**Highest (5)**	**Average**
	(percent of all survey households)					
Sugar						
Egypt	84.7	79.7	83.5	74.5	67.6	77.3
Metropolitan	81.2	81.0	84.0	65.8	63.2	72.9
Other urban	87.4	77.1	79.9	76.3	63.4	74.7
Rural	85.0	80.3	84.8	77.6	74.7	80.6
Cooking oil						
Egypt	81.6	79.1	81.9	73.4	66.1	75.8
Metropolitan	76.8	79.3	80.0	67.1	61.3	71.0
Other urban	86.4	77.8	81.8	75.1	61.5	74.1
Rural	81.7	79.5	82.5	75.3	73.9	78.7

Source: IFPRI Food Security Research Project in Egypt, "Egypt Integrated Household Survey, 1997."

Table 5.16—Per capita monthly absolute benefits to consumers from subsidized and rationed sugar and cooking oil, by region and expenditure quintile

	Per capita expenditure quintile					
Commodity/Region	**Lowest (1)**	**(2)**	**(3)**	**(4)**	**Highest (5)**	**Average**
	(LE/person/month)					
Sugar						
Egypt	0.59	0.65	0.63	0.64	0.70	0.64
Metropolitan	0.71	0.78	0.69	0.66	0.74	0.72
Other urban	0.58	0.69	0.63	0.66	0.68	0.65
Rural	0.54	0.60	0.62	0.61	0.68	0.61
Cooking oil						
Egypt	0.31	0.34	0.34	0.35	0.39	0.35
Metropolitan	0.46	0.57	0.50	0.49	0.54	0.51
Other urban	0.30	0.37	0.37	0.36	0.37	0.36
Rural	0.24	0.26	0.28	0.28	0.32	0.28

Source: IFPRI Food Security Research Project in Egypt, "Egypt Integrated Household Survey 1997."

Figure 5.9—Share of all households purchasing rationed commodities, all Egypt by expenditure quintile

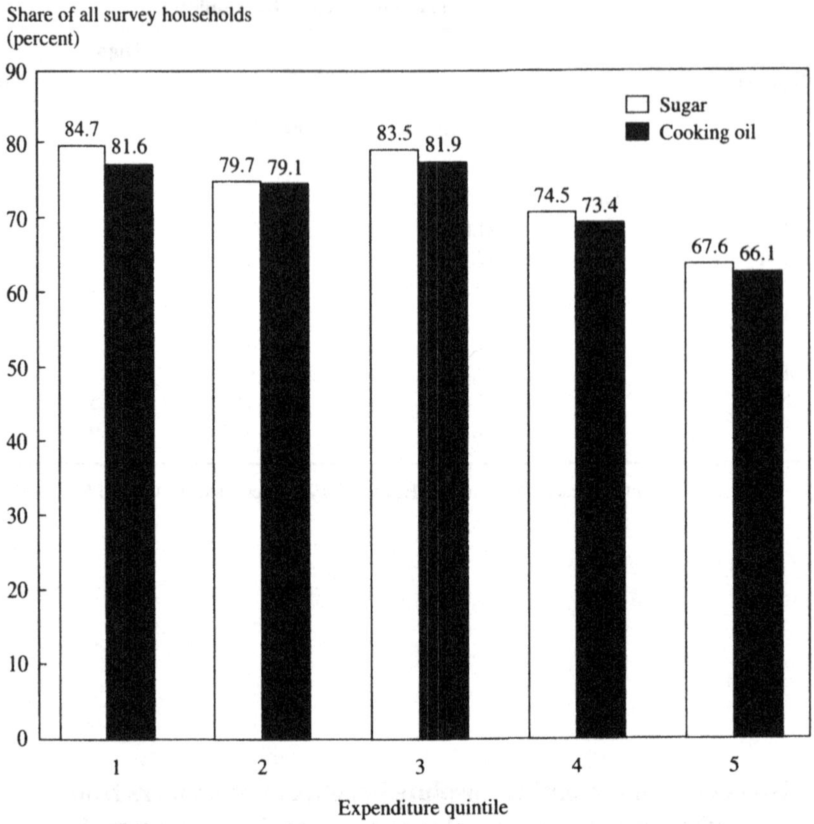

Source: Table 5.15.
Note: One is the lowest quintile and five is the highest.

Income Transfers from Food Subsidies as a Percent of Total Expenditures

Table 5.17 aggregates the income transfers from all four subsidized foods (shown in Tables 5.6 and 5.16) and provides a comparison of the total value per capita of these income transfers to total household expenditures per capita. This gives a good indication of how important food subsidies are to overall household income.

First, it should be noted that total income transfers are about 45 percent higher in urban areas than in rural areas. These demand-side figures, then, are consistent with the supply-side analysis presented earlier in this chapter, demonstrating urban bias. Second, the absolute level of subsidies is more or less constant across the first four expenditure quintiles within metropolitan, other urban, and rural areas. Therefore, the drop in the level of income transfers is noticeable for the richest quintile in the

Figure 5.10–Per capita monthly absolute benefits to consumers from rationed subsidies, all Egypt by expenditure quintile

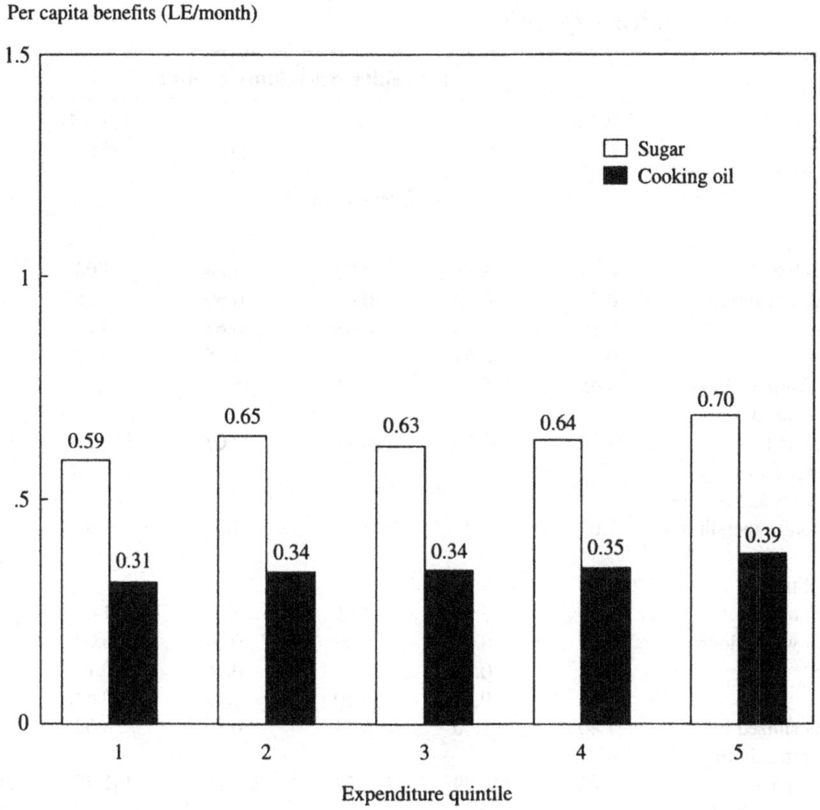

Source: Table 5.16.
Note: One is the lowest quintile and five is the highest.

metropolitan and other urban areas, but it increases noticeably for the richest quintile in rural areas. What this means for Egypt as a whole is that all income groups participate about equally in the food subsidy system in absolute terms. The system is slightly progressive in urban areas (but not decisively so) and slightly regressive in rural areas.

Third, because total expenditures increase significantly at higher quintiles, the *percentage* contribution to income of income transfers as a result of food subsidies declines monotonically with income in metropolitan, other urban, and rural areas. That is, as is to be expected, income transfers are more important to low-income households than to high-income households. For the lowest income quintiles in the metropolitan, other urban, and rural areas, income transfers from food subsidies are 7.6 percent, 8.0 percent, and 6.1 percent of total expenditures, respectively. These percentages decline to 1.2 percent, 1.6 percent, and 2.1 percent for the highest-

Table 5.17—Per capita monthly absolute benefits to consumers from all four subsidized commodities, and total benefits expressed as a percent of total per capita expenditures, by region and expenditure quintile

	Per capita expenditure quintile					
Region/Item	Lowest (1)	(2)	(3)	(4)	Highest (5)	Average
	(LE/person/month)					
Egypt						
Baladi bread	4.14	3.58	3.92	3.84	4.08	3.91
Baladi wheat flour	0.41	0.70	0.62	0.60	0.45	0.56
Sugar	0.59	0.65	0.63	0.64	0.70	0.64
Oil	0.31	0.34	0.34	0.35	0.39	0.35
All subsidized foods	5.45	5.27	5.51	5.43	5.62	5.22
Total expenditures per capita	77.44	102.16	126.74	180.07	356.18	178.97
Total food subsidy benefits as a percent of total expenditures	7.0	5.2	4.3	3.0	1.6	3.1
Metropolitan						
Baladi bread	6.23	6.05	4.95	5.02	4.40	5.22
Baladi wheat flour	0.00	0.00	0.00	0.00	0.00	0.00
Sugar	0.71	0.78	0.69	0.66	0.74	0.72
Oil	0.46	0.57	0.50	0.49	0.54	0.51
All subsidized foods	7.40	7.40	6.14	6.86	5.68	6.45
Total expenditures per capita	97.08	143.49	170.55	234.26	481.30	256.53
Total food subsidy benefits as a percent of total expenditures	7.6	5.2	3.6	2.9	1.2	2.5
Other urban						
Baladi bread	5.50	4.98	5.24	4.93	4.54	4.95
Baladi wheat flour	0.30	0.33	0.52	0.35	0.30	0.35
Sugar	0.58	0.69	0.63	0.66	0.68	0.65
Oil	0.30	0.37	0.37	0.36	0.37	0.36
All subsidized foods	6.68	6.37	6.76	6.30	5.89	6.31
Total expenditures per capita	83.77	110.19	138.46	189.78	377.79	210.20
Total food subsidy benefits as a percent of total expenditures	8.0	5.8	4.9	3.3	1.6	3.0

(continued)

Table 5.17—Continued

Region/Item	Per capita expenditure quintile Lowest (1)	(2)	(3)	(4)	Highest (5)	Average
			(LE/person/month)			
Rural						
Baladi bread	2.62	2.30	3.10	2.55	3.41	2.78
Baladi wheat flour	0.65	1.05	0.83	1.07	0.92	0.91
Sugar	0.54	0.60	0.62	0.61	0.68	0.61
Oil	0.24	0.26	0.28	0.28	0.32	0.28
All subsidized foods	4.05	4.21	4.83	4.51	5.33	4.58
Total expenditures per capita	65.87	86.35	110.07	147.21	248.26	128.36
Total food subsidy benefits as a percent of total expenditures	6.1	4.9	4.4	3.1	2.1	3.6

Source: IFPRI Food Security Research Project in Egypt, "Egypt Integrated Household Survey, 1997."

income quintile. Because incomes are lower in rural areas than in urban areas, the percentage contribution of food subsidies to total income is actually somewhat higher in rural areas than in urban areas, despite the channeling of more subsidized food to urban areas. For Egypt as a whole, income transfers from food subsidies are 3.1 percent of total expenditures per capita.

Finally, it should be noted that the demand-side data summarized in Table 5.17 (based on the EIHS surveys) indicate that subsidized *baladi* bread accounts for 72 percent of all income transfers from food subsidies for Egypt as a whole, about 80 percent in the metropolitan and other urban areas, and about 60 percent in rural areas. Two points may be made here, one technical and one with political implications. First, technically, this is quite consistent with the supply-side analysis of costs provided by MOTS, which attributed 62 percent of total costs to subsidized *baladi* bread. The demand-side percentage for subsidized *baladi* bread is of similar magnitude, but nevertheless higher than the supply-side figure, because leakage is significantly lower for subsidized *baladi* bread than for subsidized *baladi* wheat flour and rationed sugar and cooking oil. The analysis for leakage will be presented in Chapter 6. Second, subsidized *baladi* bread is overwhelmingly the most important food among the four subsidized foods in its contribution to household incomes in Egypt. Therefore, reforms related to subsidized *baladi* bread are inherently sensitive.

How does the current incidence of income transfers from food subsidies compare with the one that prevailed in the early 1980s? A comprehensive study of the Egyptian food subsidy system conducted by IFPRI in 1981/82 provides the pattern of income transfers from food subsidies in that period (Alderman and von Braun 1984). In that study, the income transfers (in terms of explicit food subsidies) from government channels showed a clear urban bias, and the magnitude of the bias was somewhat higher than that found in the current system: urban consumers received 51 percent higher income transfers than rural consumers in 1981/82. However, the income transfers were considerably higher in that period in both relative and absolute terms. The average total income transfers from food subsidies from all government channels accounted for 6.8 percent of the average total household expenditures in urban areas in 1981/82 and 7.8 percent in rural areas, while these shares in 1997 were 2.8 percent in urban areas and 3.6 percent in rural areas. In 1981/82, the average per capita transfer per month, adjusted for inflation and expressed in 1997 prices, were LE 13.54 in urban Egypt and LE 8.99 in rural Egypt. These were about twice as high as the average transfers in 1997 of LE 6.55 and LE 4.58 in urban and rural areas, respectively. This difference is mainly because more foods were included in the subsidy system in the early 1980s. Also, because *fino* and *shami* breads and 72 percent- and 76 percent-extraction wheat flour were subsidized in the early 1980s (in addition to *baladi* bread and 82 percent-extraction flour), the average income transfers from bread and flour subsidies were LE 7.73 and LE 5.59 (in 1997 prices) per capita per month, respectively, in urban and rural areas. These transfers were 44 percent and 51 percent higher than the average income transfers from bread and flour subsidies in urban and rural areas, respectively, in 1997.

CHAPTER 6

Leakage, Targeting, and Cost-Effectiveness

The analysis in this chapter indicates that the program could be improved by limiting leakage, raising targeting efficiency, and increasing cost-effectiveness. Leakage is defined here as the amount of subsidized foods that disappear at the wholesale level, never reaching the consumer. Targeting efficiency indicates the extent to which food subsidy benefits are received by the needy versus the nonneedy population. Analysis of the cost-effectiveness of the subsidy system provides estimates on the cost of government income transfers to poor consumers through the subsidy system. The analysis, which indicates relatively high leakage for *baladi* flour and for subsidized oil and sugar, suggests that there is room for program improvement.

Leakages

In any food subsidy system, the incentive exists for diverting relatively inexpensive subsidized foods for sale at a higher price in the black market or on the open market. To the extent that such leakages occur, the government incurs the cost of the subsidy, while the benefits accrue, not to the intended consumers, but to those who gain access to and sell the subsidized foods at a higher price. Depending on the rules and operation of a particular food subsidy program, leakages may occur at several points in the distribution system.

It is the task of the government to identify and minimize these leakages where they occur, taking care, however, that monitoring and enforcement costs do not exceed the benefits of reducing the leakage. Where leakages, monitoring, and enforcement costs are prohibitive, the rules and operation of the system may need to be modified or consideration given to eliminating the subsidy on the food item that has a high rate of leakage. One of the first steps in the process of evaluating performance of any food subsidy system, then, is to identify the magnitude of system leakages, that is, to determine how much of the subsidized food is being diverted before it reaches the intended consumers.

Because of the high rates of price subsidy on food items in the Egyptian system, the incentive to divert subsidized foods to the free market is quite strong. For example, private bakers receive their subsidized wheat flour (82 percent extraction) in the form of a daily quota of sacks. They pay LE 290 per metric ton for the flour. Unsubsidized wheat flour (72 percent extraction) sells on the open market for LE 1,000–1,200 per metric ton. Even the market price of bran (more than LE 400 per metric ton) is much higher than the price the bakers pay for the subsidized flour. The incentive certainly exists, then, for bakers to sift the subsidized flour into 72 percent-extraction flour and bran for sale on the open market. The extent of this specific type of illegal activity, however, is constrained by the threat of sanctions imposed by the government.

Based on the cost calculations and estimated returns, this report suggests that bakeries producing subsidized *baladi* bread are profitable enterprises, even without earning extra profit by diverting subsidized flour to the black market (see Appendix B). The estimated annual return on investment for the bakeries is quite high (61.2 percent), compared with the interest rate on loans for commercial purposes (14 percent).

Estimation Method and Data

The magnitude of leakages in the Egyptian food subsidy system can be approximated by subtracting the total quantities of subsidized *baladi* bread (wheat flour equivalent), wheat flour, sugar, and cooking oil that were actually purchased by consumers during the household survey in March–May 1997 (derived from the EIHS data) from the quantities of these commodities that MOTS placed into the system during the same period (derived from the IFPRI community survey data). The difference between supply and purchases measures the extent of leakage in the system. This method of estimating leakages as a residual has been used in studies on general food subsidy systems in other countries (Ahluwalia 1993; Rajagopalan 1989; Alderman, Chaudhry, and Garcia 1988). The methodology detailing the procedure for estimating leakages in the Egyptian food subsidy system is given in Appendix C.

Leakage Estimates

Tables 6.1, 6.2, 6.3, and 6.4 show per capita purchases of subsidized *baladi* bread, wheat flour, sugar, and cooking oil, respectively, in the five regions. Table 6.1 also shows the average weights of loaves of *baladi* bread, which were used in the calculation of leakage in the *baladi* bread subsidy system, as described in the methodology in Appendix C. Tables 6.5, 6.6, 6.7, and 6.8 estimate the leakages for subsidized *baladi* bread, wheat flour, sugar, and cooking oil, respectively, by region. Leakage estimates for Lower and Upper Egypt were not separated by urban and rural categories because many rural residents commute to neighboring urban centers for employment or trade, and they purchase subsidized foods (particularly *baladi* bread) from urban outlets. To the extent that such practices occur and provided the leakages

Table 6.1—Purchases of subsidized *baladi* bread

Region	Households purchasing subsidized *baladi* bread	Loaves of *baladi* bread purchased: Average for those who purchased	Average for all	Average weight of loaves[a]
	(percent)	(number/person/day)		(grams/loaf)
Egypt	69.4	2.7	1.9	126.1
Metropolitan	92.5	2.9	2.6	124.2
Lower urban	87.6	3.2	2.8	125.5
Lower rural	58.5	2.5	1.4	125.9
Upper urban	79.1	2.7	2.2	129.0
Upper rural	52.8	2.6	1.4	127.4

Sources: IFPRI Food Security Research Project in Egypt, "Egypt Integrated Household Survey, 1997," and "Egypt Community Survey, 1997."

[a] In the community survey, enumerators bought loaves of *baladi* bread from bakeries and then measured the weights using weighing scales. According to government specifications, each loaf of bread should weigh 130 grams.

were estimated separately for urban and rural areas, an underestimate of leakage in rural areas and an overestimate of leakage in urban areas results.

The results of the calculations suggest that leakages for subsidized *baladi* bread at the national level were quite low—11.8 percent of the total supply (Table 6.5). In contrast, estimated national average leakages for subsidized wheat flour were 27.8 percent of the supply (Table 6.6). In Lower Egypt, as much as 44.7 percent of the total supply of subsidized wheat flour appears to have been diverted, compared with 21.9 percent in Upper Egypt.

Table 6.2—Purchases of subsidized wheat flour

Region	Household purchasing subsidized wheat flour	Average quantity purchased: Average for those who purchased	Average for all
	(percent)	(kilograms/person/month)	
Egypt	21.1	5.2	1.2
Metropolitan	0.0	0.0	0.0
Lower urban	7.8	4.2	0.3
Lower rural	15.8	6.2	1.0
Upper urban	19.1	7.4	1.4
Upper rural	50.8	7.3	3.7

Source: IFPRI Food Security Research Project in Egypt, "Egypt Integrated Household Survey, 1997."

Table 6.3—Purchases of subsidized rationed sugar

Region	Household purchasing subsidized sugar	Average quantity purchased: Average for those who purchased	Average quantity purchased: Average for all
	(percent)	(kilograms/person/month)	
Egypt	77.7	0.87	0.67
Metropolitan	72.9	0.98	0.71
Lower urban	74.1	0.87	0.65
Lower rural	80.7	0.85	0.68
Upper urban	75.4	0.90	0.68
Upper rural	80.5	0.79	0.64

Source: IFPRI Food Security Research Project in Egypt, "Egypt Integrated Household Survey, 1997."

The estimated national average leakage for sugar was 19.6 percent and for cooking oil, 15.4 percent (Tables 6.7 and 6.8). In the metropolitan region, leakages in both sugar and cooking oil were relatively high (40.8 percent for sugar and 47.0 percent for cooking oil). In Upper Egypt, however, very little subsidized sugar, only 2.9 percent of its total supply, disappeared as leakage.

This analysis suggests that signi cant shares of the food subsidy bene ts were misappropriated in the distribution system before reaching the consumers. How much did these leakages cost the government? In 1997, the total cost of leakages in the Egyptian food subsidy system amounted to LE 582.8 million or 15.6 percent of the total cost of food subsidies, of which *baladi* bread accounted for 46.7 percent; wheat flour, 26.6 percent; sugar, 16.5 percent; and cooking oil, 10.2 percent.

Table 6.4—Purchases of subsidized rationed cooking oil

Region	Household purchasing subsidized cooking oil	Average quantity purchased: Average for those who purchased	Average quantity purchased: Average for all
	(percent)	(kilograms/person/month)	
Egypt	76.1	0.32	0.25
Metropolitan	71.0	0.49	0.35
Lower urban	73.3	0.31	0.23
Lower rural	77.9	0.27	0.21
Upper urban	75.1	0.37	0.28
Upper rural	79.9	0.25	0.20

Source: IFPRI Food Security Research Project in Egypt, "Egypt Integrated Household Survey, 1997."

Table 6.5—Leakage in the *baladi* bread subsidy system

Region	Flour supply to bakeries in survey areas	Flour equivalent of bread purchased by survey households	Leakage
	(grams/person/day)		(percent)
Egypt	235	201	11.8
Metropolitan	290	252	13.1
Lower	219	200	8.7
Upper	207	176	15.0

Sources: Subsidized flour supply data obtained from the Ministry of Trade and Supply; subsidized *baladi* bread purchase data are taken from the IFPRI Food Security Research Project in Egypt, "Egypt Integrated Household Survey, 1997."

Targeting Efficiency

One important advantage of a general food subsidy program such as Egypt's is that a maximum coverage of the population can be achieved without requiring an administrative structure to identify which people are eligible for subsidies. However, a major drawback of such an untargeted system is that the government must absorb the costs of providing subsidies to those who may not be in need (often referred to as "leakage" to the nonneedy).

What proportions of food subsidy benefits in Egypt go to the needy and the nonneedy? To answer this question, the needy and nonneedy populations must first be identified. The proportion of the population living below a competently drawn

Table 6.6—Leakage in the wheat flour subsidy system

Region	Subsidized flour supplied to warehouses in survey areas	Subsidized flour purchased by survey households	Leakage
	(kilogram/person/month)		(percent)
Egypt	1.52	1.22	27.8
Metropolitan	0.00	0.00	. . .
Lower	1.23	0.68	44.7
Upper	3.19	2.49	21.9

Sources: Subsidized flour supply data obtained from the Ministry of Trade and Supply; subsidized flour purchase data taken from the IFPRI Food Security Research Project in Egypt, "Egypt Integrated Household Survey, 1997."

Note: Ellipsis (. . .) indicates not applicable.

Table 6.7—Leakage in the rationed sugar subsidy system

Region	Supply of sugar in survey areas	Purchase of sugar by survey households	Leakage
	(kilogram/person/month)		(percent)
Egypt	0.91	0.67	19.6
Metropolitan	1.20	0.71	40.8
Lower	0.89	0.67	24.7
Upper	0.68	0.66	2.9

Sources: Subsidized sugar supply data obtained from the Ministry of Trade and Supply; and subsidized sugar purchase data are taken from the IFPRI Food Security Research Project in Egypt, "Egypt Integrated Household Survey, 1997."

poverty line is obviously needy. However, households just above a poverty line may also be considered deserving of food subsidies.

Recent head-count poverty measures in Egypt have varied widely. The INP (1996) study suggests that 22.9 percent of the Egyptian population were poor in 1995/96. Cardiff (1997) suggests that this figure should be 44.5 percent in 1995/96, while IFPRI's own study finds that 26.5 percent of the Egyptian population were below the poverty line in 1997 (Datt, Jolliffe, and Sharma 1998). Moreover, regional poverty measures also vary substantially within and between these studies. In this analysis, the bottom two expenditure quintiles (40 percent of the population) are considered needy, while the top three quintiles (60 percent of the population) are considered nonneedy. This type of categorization based on income or expenditure groups of the population to evaluate the efficiency of food subsidy targeting has been commonly

Table 6.8—Leakage in the rationed cooking oil subsidy system

Region	Supply of subsidized cooking oil in survey areas	Purchase of subsidized cooking oil by survey households	Leakage
	(kilogram/person/month)		(percent)
Egypt	0.36	0.25	15.4
Metropolitan	0.66	0.35	47.0
Lower	0.24	0.22	8.3
Upper	0.26	0.24	7.7

Sources: Subsidized cooking oil supply data obtained from the Ministry of Trade and Supply; subsidized cooking oil purchase data are taken from the IFPRI Food Security Research Project in Egypt, "Egypt Integrated Household Survey, 1997."

used in other studies (see Tuck and Lindert 1996; Grosh 1994; Ahluwalia 1993; Alderman, Chaudhry, and Garcia 1988).

Tables 6.9 through 6.12 show the distribution of food subsidy benefits between needy and nonneedy populations for *baladi* bread, *baladi* wheat flour, sugar, and cooking oil, by per capita expenditure quintile and region. At the national level, there is a one-to-one correspondence across income groups between the percentage of population and the percentage of benefits received from food subsidies taken as a whole. That is, 1 percent of the population receives more or less about 1 percent of the subsidy benefits, irrespective of per capita household income.

In the metropolitan region, the *baladi* bread subsidy is somewhat progressive—the richest 27 percent of the population receives 23 percent of total benefits from the *baladi* bread subsidy, while the poorest 21 percent receives 25 percent. Distribution of the benefits of the *baladi* wheat flour subsidy in the upper urban region is even more progressive—the richest 31 percent of the population receives only 18 percent of the total benefits, while the poorest 25 percent receives 29 percent. However, per capita benefits from the wheat flour subsidy are small in size.

Overall distribution of benefits from both sugar and cooking oil is slightly regressive. For Egypt, the poorest 20 percent of the population receives 18 percent of total benefits from both sugar and cooking oil, while the richest 20 percent receives 22 percent from sugar and 23 percent from cooking oil.

The overall pattern of distribution of food subsidy benefits among income groups in the present system is quite similar to the one that prevailed in the early 1980s. A comprehensive study of the Egyptian food subsidy system carried out by IFPRI in 1981/82 demonstrated that food subsidy benefits were about equally distributed across income groups during that period (Alderman and von Braun 1984).

Given that the Egyptian food subsidy system is mostly untargeted, the evidence that the distribution of benefits is not skewed toward any particular income group is not surprising. However, this pattern also suggests that a significant proportion of subsidy benefits accrues to the nonneedy. As a result, the present food subsidy system in Egypt represents an expensive means of improving food security and nutrition of the poor.

The value of total benefits from the food subsidy system going to the nonneedy is estimated to be LE 1,933.5 million, or about one-half of total food subsidy costs in 1997.[32] Combining the system leakage with targeting inefficiency, the results reveal that only about one-third of the total food subsidy paid for by the government (LE 1,224.4 million in 1997) goes to the needy, of which benefits from *baladi* bread account for 64.9 percent; wheat flour, 12.8 percent; sugar, 12.2 percent; and cooking oil, 10.1 percent.

---

[32] The value of benefits to the nonneedy is calculated after subtracting the cost of system leakage from total food subsidy costs.

Table 6.9—Per capita monthly *baladi* bread subsidy benefits accruing to expenditure quintile groups, by region, and benefits to nonneedy, 1997

Region/Item	Per capita expenditure quintile						
	Lowest (1)	(2)	(3)	(4)	Highest (5)	Average	Benefits to nonneedy[a]
							(percent)
Egypt							
Absolute benefits (LE)	4.14	3.58	3.92	3.84	4.08	3.91	
Percent of total benefits	21	18	20	20	21	. . .	61
Percent of population	20	20	20	20	20	. . .	
Metropolitan							
Absolute benefits (LE)	6.23	6.05	4.95	5.02	4.40	5.22	
Percent of total benefits within region[b]	25	15	16	21	23	. . .	60
Percent of total benefits nationally[c]	22	16	14	20	19	18	
Percent of population within region[b]	21	13	17	22	27	. . .	
Percent of population nationally[c]	13	8	10	14	17	13	
Lower urban							
Absolute benefits (LE)	5.46	5.59	6.12	5.69	4.98	5.50	
Percent of total benefits within region[b]	23	19	19	18	21	. . .	58
Percent of total benefits nationally[c]	22	21	18	19	19	20	
Percent of population within region[b]	24	18	17	18	23	. . .	
Percent of population nationally[c]	15	12	11	11	15	13	
Lower rural							
Absolute benefits (LE)	2.22	2.40	3.18	2.86	3.57	2.86	
Percent of total benefits within region[b]	18	17	24	20	22	. . .	65
Percent of total benefits nationally[c]	19	22	26	23	23	23	
Percent of population within region[b]	23	20	21	19	17	. . .	
Percent of population nationally[c]	33	29	30	28	25	29	
Upper urban							
Absolute benefits (LE)	5.59	3.89	4.15	4.32	4.10	4.30	
Percent of total benefits within region[b]	16	12	18	24	30	. . .	72
Percent of total benefits nationally[c]	12	11	14	20	21	16	
Percent of population within region[b]	12	13	19	24	31	. . .	

(continued)

Table 6.9—Continued

Region/Item	Per capita expenditure quintile Lowest (1)	(2)	(3)	(4)	Highest (5)	Average	Benefits to nonneedy[a]
							(percent)
Percent of population nationally[c]	8	9	13	16	21	13	
Upper rural							
Absolute benefits (LE)	3.15	2.18	2.99	2.09	3.15	2.67	
Percent of total benefits within region[b]	22	21	25	15	17	. . .	57
Percent of total benefits nationally[c]	25	29	28	19	18	24	
Percent of population within region[b]	19	26	22	19	14	. . .	
Percent of population nationally[c]	30	42	35	31	23	32	

Source: IFPRI Food Security Research Project in Egypt, "Egypt Integrated Household Survey, 1997."

Notes: Absolute benefits are calculated as follows:

(1) Per capita purchased quantity of loaves of subsidized *baladi* bread for each quintile is multiplied by the full cost of LE 0.116 per loaf of bread.

(2) Full cost is multiplied by the rate of subsidy (0.569) to obtain per capita subsidy benefit (or income transfer).

Ellipsis (. . .) indicates not applicable.

[a] Poor and low-income families belonging to quintiles 1 and 2 (bottom 40 percent of the population) are considered needy.

[b] "Within region" indicates that percentages sum to 100 percent across each respective row.

[c] "Nationally" indicates that percentages sum to 100 percent within each expenditure quintile column across regions.

Cost-Effectiveness

At what cost does the government transfer income to needy consumers through food subsidies? An evaluation of the cost-effectiveness of a consumer-oriented food subsidy program involves a comparison of costs of the program for providing measured benefits to needy consumers. The fiscal costs of food subsidy programs consist of direct food costs and administrative costs for operating the system. Revenue generated from the sale of food at a subsidized price is deducted from costs. Benefits are measured by the income transfer (subsidy) received from the program by the consumers. Any pilferage or leakage represents a system loss and, therefore, is not counted in the calculation of benefits.

In this study, the cost-effectiveness analysis is carried out for subsidized *baladi* bread, wheat flour, sugar, and cooking oil. Subsidy costs for each of the four items

Table 6.10—Per capita monthly wheat flour subsidy benefits accruing to expenditure quintile groups, by region, and benefits to nonneedy, 1997

	Per capita expenditure quintile						
Region/Item	Lowest (1)	(2)	(3)	(4)	Highest (5)	Average	Benefits to nonneedy[a]
							(percent)
Egypt							
Absolute benefits (LE)	0.41	0.70	0.62	0.60	0.45	0.56	
Percent of total benefits	15	25	22	22	16	. . .	60
Percent of population	20	20	20	20	20	. . .	
Metropolitan							
Absolute benefits (LE)	0.00	0.00	0.00	0.00	0.00	0.00	
Percent of population within region[b]	21	13	17	22	27	. . .	
Percent of population nationally[c]	13	8	10	14	17	13	
Lower urban							
Absolute benefits (LE)	0.10	0.12	0.04	0.14	0.23	0.14	
Percent of total benefits within region[b]	18	17	5	19	40	. . .	65
Percent of total benefits nationally[c]	3	2	1	2	6	2	
Percent of population within region[b]	24	18	17	18	23	. . .	
Percent of population nationally[c]	15	12	11	11	15	13	
Lower rural							
Absolute benefits (LE)	0.35	0.54	0.34	0.35	0.55	0.42	
Percent of total benefits within region[b]	19	26	17	16	22	. . .	55
Percent of total benefits nationally[c]	23	17	13	12	23	17	
Percent of population within region[b]	23	20	21	19	17	. . .	
Percent of population nationally[c]	33	29	30	28	25	29	
Upper urban							
Absolute benefits (LE)	0.71	0.71	1.13	0.51	0.36	0.60	
Percent of total benefits within region[b]	14	15	34	19	18	. . .	74
Percent of total benefits nationally[c]	12	7	18	10	12	11	
Percent of population within region[b]	12	13	19	24	31	. . .	
Percent of population nationally[c]	8	9	13	16	21	13	
Upper rural							
Absolute benefits (LE)	1.04	1.64	1.58	2.11	1.53	1.59	

(continued)

Table 6.10—Continued

Region/Item	Lowest (1)	(2)	(3)	(4)	Highest (5)	Average	Benefits to nonneedy[a]
							(percent)
Percent of total benefits within region[b]	12	27	22	26	14	. . .	61
Percent of total benefits nationally[c]	62	75	69	77	59	70	
Percent of population within region[b]	19	26	22	19	14	. . .	
Percent of population nationally[c]	30	42	35	31	23	32	

Source: IFPRI Food Security Research Project in Egypt, "Egypt Integrated Household Survey, 1997."

Notes: Absolute benefits are calculated as follows:

(1) Per capita purchased quantity of subsidized wheat flour for each quintile is multiplied by the full cost of LE 0.966 per kilogram of wheat flour.

(2) Full cost is multiplied by the rate of subsidy (0.431) to obtain per capita subsidy benefit (or income transfer).

Ellipsis (. . .) indicates not applicable.

[a] Poor and low-income families belonging to quintiles 1 and 2 (bottom 40 percent of the population) are considered needy.

[b] "Within region" indicates that percentages sum to 100 percent across each respective row.

[c] "Nationally" indicates that percentages sum to 100 percent within each expenditure quintile column across regions.

are calculated from data for 1996/97 obtained from MOTS. Appendix A describes the method of calculating food subsidy costs and, as an example, shows in detail how the subsidy costs were calculated for the 1996/97 *baladi* bread subsidy program.

Two sets of subsidy benefits have been estimated for each of the four subsidized foods. Since the Egyptian food subsidies are untargeted, in the first set, the income transfer to any consumer in general is estimated. Here, only the system leakage (or pilferage before the subsidies reach the consumers) is deducted from income transfers. In the second set, income transfers only to the needy[33] population are calculated by subtracting system leakage as well as benefits accruing to the nonneedy from income transfers.

On the basis of the two sets of income transfer estimates (that is, for general consumers and for the needy), two sets of cost-effectiveness estimates have been made for each of the four subsidized foods (Appendix F, Table F.9). In the first set, cost-

[33] The lowest two expenditure quintiles (bottom 40 percent of the population) are defined as needy.

Table 6.11—Per capita monthly sugar subsidy benefits accruing to expenditure quintile groups, by region, and benefits to nonneedy, 1997

Region/Item	Per capita expenditure quintile						Benefits to nonneedy[a]
	Lowest (1)	(2)	(3)	(4)	Highest (5)	Average	(percent)
Egypt							
Absolute benefits (LE)	0.59	0.65	0.63	0.64	0.70	0.64	
Percent of total benefits	18	20	20	20	22	. . .	62
Percent population	20	20	20	20	20	. . .	
Metropolitan							
Absolute benefits (LE)	0.71	0.78	0.69	0.66	0.74	0.72	
Percent of total benefits within region[b]	21	15	16	20	28	. . .	64
Percent of total benefits nationally[c]	17	11	11	14	18	14	
Percent of population within region[b]	21	13	17	22	27	. . .	
Percent of population nationally[c]	13	8	10	14	17	13	
Lower urban							
Absolute benefits (LE)	0.58	0.73	0.59	0.64	0.64	0.64	
Percent of total benefits within region[b]	22	21	16	18	23	. . .	56
Percent of total benefits nationally[c]	15	14	11	11	14	13	
Percent of population within region[b]	24	18	17	18	23	. . .	
Percent of population nationally[c]	15	12	11	11	15	13	
Lower rural							
Absolute benefits (LE)	0.56	0.62	0.64	0.67	0.69	0.63	
Percent of total benefits within region[b]	20	19	21	21	19	. . .	61
Percent of total benefits nationally[c]	33	29	31	30	25	29	
Percent of population within region[b]	23	20	21	19	17	. . .	
Percent of population nationally[c]	33	29	30	28	25	29	
Upper urban							
Absolute benefits (LE)	0.59	0.61	0.68	0.68	0.72	0.67	
Percent of total benefits within region[b]	11	12	19	24	34	. . .	77
Percent of total benefits nationally[c]	8	9	14	17	21	14	
Percent of population within region[b]	12	13	19	24	31	. . .	

(continued)

Table 6.11—Continued

Region/Item	Lowest (1)	(2)	(3)	(4)	Highest (5)	Average	Benefits to nonneedy[a]
							(percent)
Percent of population nationally[c]	8	9	13	16	21	13	
Upper rural							
Absolute benefits (LE)	0.51	0.57	0.59	0.56	0.66	0.58	
Percent of total benefits within region[b]	16	26	23	19	16	. . .	58
Percent of total benefits nationally[c]	27	38	33	28	22	30	
Percent of population within region[b]	19	26	22	19	14	. . .	
Percent of population nationally[c]	30	42	35	31	23	32	

Per capita expenditure quintile (columns 1–5).

Source: IFPRI Food Security Research Project in Egypt, "Egypt Integrated Household Survey, 1997."

Notes: Absolute benefits are calculated as follows:

(1) Per capita purchased quantity of subsidized sugar for each quintile is multiplied by the full cost of LE 1.32 per kilogram of sugar.

(2) Full cost is multiplied by the rate of subsidy for green ration card (0.621) and for red ration card (0.432). Benefits per capita represent the weighted average of proportions of the users of green and red ration cards in each expenditure quintile group.

Ellipsis (. . .) indicates not applicable.

[a] Poor and low-income families belonging to quintiles 1 and 2 (bottom 40 percent of the population) are considered needy.

[b] "Within region" indicates that percentages sum to 100 percent across each respective row.

[c] "Nationally" indicates that percentages sum to 100 percent within each expenditure quintile column across regions.

effectiveness is estimated by dividing the subsidy cost by the income transfers received by general consumers, which represents the cost of supplying LE 1.00 of income to general consumers. In the second set, cost-effectiveness is estimated by dividing the same subsidy cost by the income transfer received only by the needy. This represents the cost of supplying LE 1.00 income to the needy, if the goal is to reach only the bottom 40 percent of the population. If food subsidies are intended only for the needy, then the government bears the cost of leakage to households in the richest three quintiles. The cost of supplying subsidy benefits to the needy increases by the amount of the cost of leakage to the nonneedy.

Figure 6.1 presents the results of the cost-effectiveness analysis. Appendix Table F.9 provides the calculations for deriving these results. For each subsidized food, the costs of supplying LE 1.00 income transfer to (1) general consumers and (2) to needy consumers are shown in the figure. Among the four subsidized foods, the *baladi*

Table 6.12—Per capita monthly cooking oil subsidy benefits accruing to expenditure quintile groups, by region, and benefits to nonneedy, 1997

	Per capita expenditure quintile						
Region/Item	Lowest (1)	(2)	(3)	(4)	Highest (5)	Average	Benefits to nonneedy[a]
							(percent)
Egypt							
Absolute benefits (LE)	0.31	0.34	0.34	0.35	0.39	0.35	
Percent of total benefits	18	20	20	20	23	. . .	62
Percent population	20	20	20	20	20	. . .	
Metropolitan							
Absolute benefits (LE)	0.46	0.57	0.50	0.49	0.54	0.51	
Percent of total benefits within region[b]	19	15	16	21	29	. . .	66
Percent of total benefits nationally[c]	22	16	16	20	24	20	
Percent of population within region[b]	21	13	17	22	27	. . .	
Percent of population nationally[c]	13	8	10	14	17	13	
Lower urban							
Absolute benefits (LE)	0.28	0.38	0.34	0.33	0.33	0.33	
Percent of total benefits within region[b]	20	21	18	18	23	. . .	59
Percent of total benefits nationally[c]	15	15	12	11	13	13	
Percent of population within region[b]	24	18	17	18	23	. . .	
Percent of population nationally[c]	15	12	11	11	15	13	
Lower rural							
Absolute benefits (LE)	0.23	0.27	0.29	0.30	0.34	0.28	
Percent of total benefits within region[b]	19	19	21	21	21	. . .	62
Percent of total benefits nationally[c]	27	25	27	26	22	25	
Percent of population within region[b]	23	20	21	19	17	. . .	
Percent of population nationally[c]	33	29	30	28	25	29	
Upper urban							
Absolute benefits (LE)	0.36	0.34	0.41	0.39	0.42	0.39	
Percent of total benefits within region[b]	11	11	20	24	33	. . .	77
Percent of total benefits nationally[c]	10	10	16	19	23	16	
Percent of population within region[b]	12	13	19	24	31	. . .	

(continued)

Table 6.12—Continued

Region/Item	Per capita expenditure quintile: Lowest (1)	(2)	(3)	(4)	Highest (5)	Average	Benefits to nonneedy[a]
							(percent)
Percent of population nationally[c]	8	9	13	16	21	13	
Upper rural							
Absolute benefits (LE)	0.25	0.25	0.27	0.25	0.30	0.26	
Percent of total benefits within region[b]	18	25	23	18	16	. . .	57
Percent of total benefits nationally[c]	26	34	29	24	18	26	
Percent of population within region[b]	19	26	22	19	14	. . .	
Percent of population nationally[c]	30	42	35	31	23	32	

Source: IFPRI Food Security Research Project in Egypt, "Egypt Integrated Household Survey, 1997."

Notes: Absolute benefits are calculated as follows:

(1) Per capita purchased quantity of subsidized cooking oil for each quintile is multiplied by the full cost of LE 2.18 per kilogram of cooking oil.

(2) Full cost is multiplied by the rate of subsidy for green ration card (0.541) and for red card (0.427). Benefits per capita represent the weighted average of proportions of the users of green and red ration cards in each expenditure quintile group.

Ellipsis (. . .) indicates not applicable.

[a] Poor and low-income families belonging to quintiles 1 and 2 (bottom 40 percent of the population) are considered needy.

[b] "Within region" indicates that percentages sum to 100 percent across each respective row.

[c] "Nationally" indicates that percentages sum to 100 percent within each expenditure quintile column across regions.

bread subsidy system delivers LE 1.00 income to all consumers at a cost of LE 1.16—the lowest cost among the four subsidized foods. This low cost is directly explained by the low level of leakage for *baladi* bread. However, because 61 percent of the benefits from the *baladi* bread subsidy goes to the nonneedy, the system requires LE 2.98 to transfer LE 1.00 to a needy household.

In contrast, the rationed cooking oil subsidy proved to be the least effective at directing income to all consumers and to needy consumers as well. The oil subsidy bears the high costs associated with refining, packaging, and handling this fluid commodity. A large portion of benefits accrue to the nonneedy. Consequently, the system transfers LE 1.00 to general consumers at a cost of LE 1.76 and LE 1.00 to the needy at a cost of LE 4.64.

The intermediate performers are the sugar and wheat flour subsidy systems. The rationed sugar subsidy system requires LE 1.27 to transfer LE 1.00 to any consumer

Table 6.13—International comparison of cost-effectiveness of selective programs

Country/Program	Fiscal cost to deliver $1.00 subsidy to the needy
	($)
Egypt	
Subsidized *baladi* bread	2.98
Subsidized wheat flour	3.71
Subsidized sugar	3.34
Subsidized cooking oil	4.64
The Philippines	
Pilot food price subsidy scheme, 1984	1.19
General rice price subsidy, 1992	5.98
Brazil	
Food subsidy (PINS), 1980	1.21
Preschool feeding and nutrition education, 1980	2.38
Colombia	
Food subsidy, 1981	1.58
Indonesia	
Feeding program, 1982	2.48
Tamil Nadu, India	
Weighing and feeding, 1982	1.74
Bangladesh	
Vulnerable group development program, 1992	1.62
Food-for-work program, 1982	2.44
Food-for-education program, 1994	1.59
Rural rationing program, 1992	6.55

Sources: For Egypt, Table F.9; for pilot food price subsidy scheme in the Philippines, Garcia and Pinstrup-Andersen (1987); for general price subsidy in the Philippines, Subbarao, Ahmed, and Teklu (1996); for Brazil, Colombia, Indonesia, and India, World Bank (1984); and for Bangladesh, Ahmed and Billah (1994).

and LE 3.34 to needy consumers. The wheat flour subsidy system transfers LE 1.00 at a cost of LE 1.48 to consumers in general, and LE 1.00 to needy consumers at a cost of LE 3.71.

The total aggregate estimated benefit for all four subsidized foods that accrue to the needy was LE 1,224.4 million in 1997. The estimated fiscal or budgetary cost of food subsidies was LE 3,740.6 million in the same year. Therefore, it costs the government LE 3.06 to transfer LE 1.00 of income to a needy household through its food subsidy system.

How cost-effective are the Egyptian food subsidies in transferring income to the needy, compared with programs in other countries? The cost-effectiveness of transferring income to the needy for food-based interventions in selected countries is shown in Table 6.13. Except for the general rice price subsidy in the Philippines, all other programs were officially targeted to the needy. A comparison with the Egyp-

Figure 6.1—Cost-effectiveness of the food subsidy system (cost of supplying LE 1.00 to a consumer)

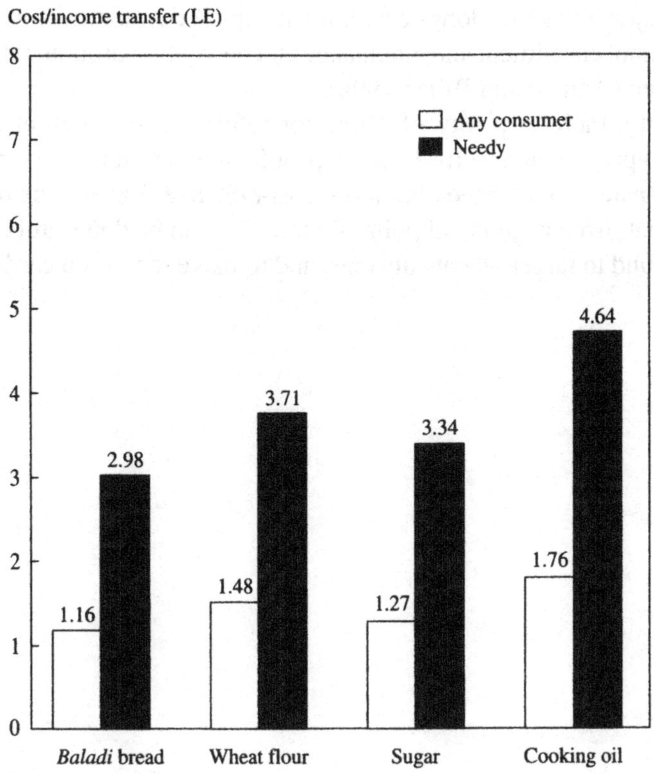

Source: Appendix F, Table F.9.

tian food subsidy system indicates that, with the exception of the Rural Rationing Program in Bangladesh, targeted programs in other countries transfer income to the needy at a lower cost than do the untargeted food subsidies in Egypt. Targeting that reduces leakage of benefits to the nonneedy is the primary reason that other programs are more cost-effective.

The rice price subsidy scheme in the Philippines transferred $1.00 of income to the poor at a cost of $5.98. In this untargeted subsidy system, the cost to provide benefits to the poor was high because a large portion of the benefits leaked to non-needy persons (Subbarao, Ahmed, and Teklu 1996). Among the four targeted food subsidy programs in Bangladesh, the Food-for-Education and the Vulnerable Group Development Programs transfer income at least cost because these programs operate with low leakages (Ahmed and Billah 1994; WGTFI 1994). In contrast, Bangladesh's Rural Rationing Program was most ineffective in transferring income to target households. It operated with enormous rates of leakage (70 percent), even though the program was administratively targeted (Ahmed 1992). Because of its poor performance in reaching the poor, the government abolished the program in 1992. In its place, the government introduced the innovative Food-for-Education Program, which proved to be a highly cost-effective income transfer program. This program also had a major impact on long-term human capital development by significantly increasing school enrollment and attendance and preventing dropout rates of primary school children (Ahmed and Billah 1994).

In summary, there is plenty of scope for reforming the present food subsidy scheme in Egypt, particularly for *baladi* wheat flour and rationed sugar and cooking oil, so that transfers to the needy are more cost-effective. Experience in other countries shows that, from a technical point of view, this can be done. But can the political will be found to target wheat subsidies and to make the ration card system more progressive?

CHAPTER 7

Patterns of Food Demand

In this chapter food consumption patterns in Upper and Lower Egypt are broken down by urban and rural areas and by income groups. Then complete demand matrixes of price and income elasticities are developed for use in policy analysis. Such matrixes can be used, for example, to project food demand. They are also essential for simulating outcomes of various policy reforms that the government may want to consider.

The analysis finds that subsidized *baladi* bread accounts for about one-half of staple food consumption in urban areas and one-quarter of staple food consumption in rural areas. Subsidized *baladi* wheat flour provides about one-fifth of the staple food consumed in rural Upper Egypt. Consumers are shown to be relatively insensitive to marginal increases in the price of subsidized *baladi* bread.

Patterns of Food Consumption by Broad Food Group

The top sections of Tables 7.1–7.5 present per capita food expenditures for each of the broad food groups by expenditure quintile for the five regions. Table 7.6 summarizes the patterns of increases in spending across expenditure quintiles and budget shares for three broad categories: cereals, nonstaple plant foods, and animal and fish products.

Budget shares for cereals are quite low, below 20 percent for the three urban regions and just above 20 percent for the two rural regions. In all regions, the remaining food expenditures are about equally divided between nonstaple plant foods and animal and fish products. The percentage of the food budget going to animal and fish products is highest in the metropolitan region where incomes are highest and lowest in the two rural regions, where incomes are lowest.

On average across all five regions, the richest income quintiles spend more than twice as much for food as the lowest income quintiles. In all five regions, expenditures for nonstaple plant foods rise at nearly the same rate as total food expenditures, so that the budget shares for nonstaple plant foods remain more or less constant across expenditure quintiles in Table 7.6. Expenditures for cereals also increase between low and high expenditure quintiles at a remarkably constant rate across the

Table 7.1—Per capita expenditures, calorie availability, and calorie cost, by food group for metropolitan Egypt, 1997

	Per capita fitted expenditure quintile					
Food group	1	2	3	4	5	All
Per capita expenditure (LE/week)						
Cereals	2.42	2.96	3.23	3.52	3.51	3.13
All noncereals	10.41	16.30	18.85	25.42	31.04	20.41
Pulses	1.08	1.16	1.10	1.30	1.15	1.16
Vegetables	1.71	2.32	2.67	3.24	3.22	2.63
Fruits	0.70	1.10	1.48	1.97	2.95	1.64
Meat	2.88	5.38	6.31	9.51	11.85	7.19
Eggs, milk	2.19	3.18	3.72	4.82	5.97	3.97
Oil	0.82	1.45	1.54	1.95	2.12	1.58
Condiments	0.13	0.21	0.26	0.32	0.39	0.26
Sugar, sweets	0.47	0.77	1.01	1.45	1.82	0.11
Beverages	0.44	0.72	0.76	0.87	1.58	0.87
All foods	12.82	19.25	22.08	28.95	34.54	23.53
Per capita calorie availability per day						
Cereals	1,454	1,620	1,617	1,707	1,597	1,599
All noncereals	1,128	1,584	1,643	2,124	2,278	1,752
Pulses	211	234	200	235	222	220
Vegetables	98	125	145	169	152	138
Fruits	44	66	87	111	138	89
Meat	109	194	215	310	393	244
Eggs, milk	173	238	266	350	424	290
Oil	307	452	417	529	495	440
Condiments	8	11	14	23	23	16
Sugar, sweets	173	239	281	379	386	291
Beverages	5	26	17	18	44	22
All foods	2,582	3,204	3,260	3,831	3,874	3,351
Calories purchased per 10 piasters (LE 0.10)						
Cereals	424	397	362	350	334	373
All noncereals	82	73	66	63	56	68
Pulses	137	147	132	128	138	136
Vegetables	43	41	40	39	36	40
Fruits	51	46	45	44	40	45
Meat	28	28	24	23	24	25
Eggs, milk	56	54	51	53	52	53
Oil	322	262	235	221	180	244
Condiments	38	38	35	56	48	43
Sugar, sweets	358	294	264	235	202	269
Beverages	6	11	13	12	14	11
All foods	151	128	116	102	89	117

Source: IFPRI Food Security Research Project in Egypt, "Egypt Integrated Household Survey, 1997."

Table 7.2—Per capita expenditures, calorie availability, and calorie cost, by food group for urban Lower Egypt, 1997

	Per capita fitted expenditure quintile					
Food group	**1**	**2**	**3**	**4**	**5**	**All**
Per capita expenditure (LE/week)						
Cereals	2.88	3.12	3.25	3.79	3.45	3.30
All noncereals	10.12	11.73	14.19	22.11	23.54	16.33
Pulses	0.91	1.01	1.10	1.24	1.24	1.10
Vegetables	1.50	1.79	2.06	2.83	2.90	2.22
Fruits	0.56	0.69	0.84	1.62	1.74	1.09
Meat	3.61	4.14	5.00	7.70	8.61	5.81
Eggs, milk	1.29	1.63	2.16	3.64	3.62	2.46
Oil	1.04	1.17	1.39	2.42	2.39	1.68
Condiments	0.13	0.21	0.21	0.31	0.31	0.23
Sugar, sweets	0.60	0.68	0.92	1.40	1.81	1.08
Beverages	0.47	0.42	0.51	0.96	0.92	0.66
All foods	13.01	14.84	17.43	25.9	26.99	19.63
Per capita calorie availability per day						
Cereals	1,674	1,801	1,839	2,072	1,834	1,844
All noncereals	1,149	1,263	1,598	2,130	2,162	1,660
Pulses	203	218	344	257	269	258
Vegetables	100	120	130	172	164	137
Fruits	40	51	61	104	107	73
Meat	135	145	165	277	257	196
Eggs, milk	137	161	212	336	315	232
Oil	329	360	421	626	608	469
Condiments	8	12	12	19	19	14
Sugar, sweets	178	193	247	320	407	269
Beverages	18	3	7	20	16	13
All foods	2,823	3,065	3,437	4,202	3,996	3,504
Calorie purchased per 10 piasters (LE 0.10)						
Cereals	422	416	409	390	383	404
All noncereals	85	76	81	69	66	75
Pulses	156	152	178	142	146	155
Vegetables	50	50	47	44	42	47
Fruits	53	54	57	48	48	52
Meat	29	27	25	25	23	26
Eggs, milk	79	74	73	68	64	72
Oil	265	249	248	227	228	243
Condiments	35	39	35	45	42	39
Sugar, sweets	262	259	233	221	226	240
Beverages	5	4	6	8	8	6
All foods	167	151	148	118	114	140

Source: IFPRI Food Security Research Project in Egypt, "Egypt Integrated Household Survey, 1997."

Table 7.3—Per capita expenditures, calorie availability, and calorie cost, by food group for rural Lower Egypt, 1997

Food group	Per capita fitted expenditure quintile					
	1	2	3	4	5	All
Per capita expenditure (LE/week)						
Cereals	2.89	3.21	3.55	3.53	4.69	3.57
All noncereals	9.33	10.40	12.77	14.78	20.04	13.46
Pulses	0.64	0.80	0.99	1.02	1.21	0.94
Vegetables	1.20	1.52	1.87	2.08	2.57	1.85
Fruits	0.36	0.48	0.73	0.93	1.50	0.80
Meat	3.99	3.25	4.12	5.23	7.10	4.74
Eggs, milk	1.21	1.75	1.94	2.21	2.97	2.02
Oil	0.97	1.37	1.65	1.71	2.24	1.59
Condiments	0.12	0.18	0.20	0.22	0.35	0.21
Sugar, sweets	0.51	0.70	0.83	0.94	1.33	0.86
Beverages	0.33	0.35	0.45	0.44	0.76	0.47
All foods	12.22	13.61	16.32	18.31	24.73	17.03
Per capita calorie availability per day						
Cereals	1,645	1,823	2,001	1,914	2,554	1,987
All noncereals	1,064	1,288	1,579	1,631	2,094	1,531
Pulses	142	182	282	227	286	224
Vegetables	98	117	131	146	173	133
Fruits	31	42	55	76	105	62
Meat	147	132	163	201	271	183
Eggs, milk	146	192	226	248	306	224
Oil	318	393	453	453	584	440
Condiments	11	16	17	18	20	16
Sugar, sweets	167	211	245	256	339	243
Beverages	3	3	7	6	12	6
All foods	2,708	3,111	3,580	3,546	4,648	3,518
Calorie purchased per 10 piasters (LE 0.10)						
Cereals	421	410	397	408	399	407
All noncereals	94	90	94	83	77	88
Pulses	163	162	218	168	191	181
Vegetables	63	57	52	52	48	54
Fruits	66	66	57	57	53	60
Meat	32	31	30	29	27	30
Eggs, milk	88	79	87	83	77	83
Oil	287	235	224	240	221	241
Condiments	60	53	50	47	38	50
Sugar, sweets	290	233	260	241	218	248
Beverages	4	4	6	5	7	5
All foods	191	171	165	157	142	165

Source: IFPRI Food Security Research Project in Egypt, "Egypt Integrated Household Survey, 1997."

Table 7.4—Per capita expenditures, calorie availability, and calorie cost, by food group for urban Upper Egypt, 1997

	Per capita fitted expenditure quintile					
Food group	1	2	3	4	5	All
Per capita food expenditure (LE/week)						
Cereals	2.61	3.03	3.2	3.35	4.07	3.25
All noncereals	11.96	15.99	22.70	22.70	34.51	21.56
Pulses	1.05	1.22	1.21	1.13	1.44	1.21
Vegetables	1.38	1.92	2.53	2.57	3.89	2.46
Fruits	0.65	0.92	1.41	1.73	3.16	1.57
Meat	4.68	5.70	9.34	8.24	12.69	8.12
Eggs, milk	1.47	2.23	3.34	3.42	5.90	3.27
Oil	1.25	1.68	2.16	2.15	3.14	2.07
Condiments	0.16	0.31	0.30	0.36	0.43	0.31
Sugar, sweets	0.86	1.14	1.42	1.86	2.15	1.48
Beverages	0.45	0.87	0.99	1.25	1.71	1.06
All foods	14.57	19.02	25.90	26.06	38.58	24.81
Per capita calorie availability per day						
Cereals	1,625	1,713	1,724	1,758	1,731	1,710
All noncereals	1,408	1,603	2,038	2,006	2,689	1,948
Pulses	320	268	248	291	277	281
Vegetables	91	116	139	132	193	134
Fruits	65	59	89	96	155	93
Meat	153	191	309	284	436	275
Eggs, milk	145	184	274	245	393	248
Oil	359	437	553	514	684	509
Condiments	11	17	24	21	28	20
Sugar, sweets	258	313	372	376	460	355
Beverages	7	17	31	45	63	32
All foods	3,033	3,316	3,762	3,764	4,420	3,658
Calories purchased per 10 piasters (LE 0.10)						
Cereals	483	411	395	370	334	399
All noncereals	99	75	67	68	60	74
Pulses	212	182	147	184	138	173
Vegetables	52	47	41	39	36	43
Fruits	59	55	53	43	41	50
Meat	23	23	23	25	24	24
Eggs, milk	83	63	58	55	49	62
Oil	245	215	213	187	188	209
Condiments	41	50	45	53	49	48
Sugar, sweets	259	233	223	181	183	216
Beverages	6	10	15	15	17	13
All foods	173	138	110	110	89	124

Source: IFPRI Food Security Research Project in Egypt, "Egypt Integrated Household Survey, 1997."

Table 7.5—Per capita expenditures, calorie availability, and calorie cost, by food group for rural Upper Egypt, 1997

	Per capita fitted expenditure quintile					
Food group	**1**	**2**	**3**	**4**	**5**	**All**
Per capita expenditure (LE/week)						
Cereals	3.11	3.24	3.25	3.75	4.50	3.57
All noncereals	7.70	10.32	12.57	14.70	23.87	13.83
Pulses	0.78	0.92	1.05	1.16	1.33	1.05
Vegetables	0.92	1.21	1.40	1.69	2.42	1.53
Fruits	0.22	0.36	0.47	0.72	1.44	0.64
Meat	2.47	3.65	4.85	5.41	10.02	5.28
Eggs, milk	0.90	1.08	1.27	1.68	2.78	1.54
Oil	1.20	1.54	1.82	1.75	2.86	1.83
Condiments	0.09	0.12	0.15	0.19	0.29	0.17
Sugar, sweets	0.75	0.96	1.04	1.44	1.74	1.18
Beverages	0.37	0.50	0.52	0.64	0.98	0.60
All foods	10.82	13.56	15.82	18.45	28.37	17.40
Per capita calorie availability per day						
Cereals	1,879	1,975	1,893	2,139	2,513	2,080
All noncereals	991	1,269	1,487	1,588	2,245	1,516
Pulses	188	225	289	254	286	248
Vegetables	70	89	98	112	145	103
Fruits	26	33	39	56	106	52
Meat	79	122	151	174	308	167
Eggs, milk	119	157	158	187	285	181
Oil	261	334	418	417	605	407
Condiments	5	9	10	15	24	13
Sugar, sweets	240	293	319	364	465	336
Beverages	3	8	5	9	21	9
All foods	2,870	3,245	3,380	3,727	4,758	3,595
Calorie purchased per 10 piasters (LE 0.10)						
Cereals	473	442	448	431	417	442
All noncereals	96	92	92	84	75	88
Pulses	164	169	206	151	147	168
Vegetables	58	55	54	48	46	52
Fruits	90	76	63	58	60	68
Meat	22	24	22	23	24	23
Eggs, milk	101	102	96	84	82	93
Oil	207	193	203	238	181	204
Condiments	31	47	41	53	52	45
Sugar, sweets	256	239	239	216	213	233
Beverages	5	7	6	7	11	7
All foods	203	185	174	160	139	172

Source: IFPRI Food Security Research Project in Egypt, "Egypt Integrated Household Survey, 1997."

five regions (although the increase is somewhat smaller in the lower urban region). However, percentage increases for cereals are smaller than those for total food, so that budget shares for cereals decline as income grows. Budget shares for animal and fish products increase as income rises (with the exception of the lower rural region where the budget share for animal and fish products remains constant).

Calorie Availability

The middle sections of Tables 7.1 to 7.5 present per capita calorie availability by expenditure quintile for the broad food groups in the five regions. Table 7.6 also summarizes the patterns of increases in calorie availability across expenditure quintiles and calorie shares for cereals, nonstaple plant foods, and animal and fish products.

Cereals contribute 47–58 percent of total calorie availability depending on the region, much higher than cereal's share of the food budget. This indicates that cereals are relatively inexpensive sources of calories. Nonstaple plant foods account for 32–39 percent of total calorie availability, which is marginally lower than the nonstaple plant food budget share. Animal and fish products make up 10–16 percent of total calorie availability—much smaller percentages than their budget shares, which indicates that animal and fish products are relatively expensive sources of calories.

Note that percentage increases in total calorie availability between the poorest and the richest quintiles are substantial in all five regions, between 42 percent and 72 percent. These percentage increases are highest in rural areas.[34] Which food groups contribute to these calorie increases? In the three urban regions, per capita cereal availability rises very little with income—much of the increase in cereal availability can be attributed to the fact that average ages in higher-income households tend to be higher (there are fewer children and more adults in richer households). Consequently, in urban areas (with household composition controlled), nonstaple plant foods and animal and fish products account for most of the increase in calorie consumption as income increases. In the two rural regions, it is a combination of increases in energy intakes from all three broad food groups (cereals, nonstaple plant foods, animal and fish products). In all five regions, then, dietary quality (increased consumption of noncereal foods) improves rapidly with increases in income.

Finally, it should be noted that all ratios in the first section of Table 7.6 (food expenditures) are greater than the corresponding ratios in the second section (calorie availability); expenditures within each of the three food groups rise faster with income than does calorie availability. This indicates more expensive sources of calories are purchased as income increases.

---

[34] It is likely that these figures overstate the actual increase in calorie *intakes* across expenditure quintiles. Two possible reasons for this are that (1) higher-income households tend to transfer food to lower-income households in the form of meals given to poorer relatives and hired workers (this is consistent with the higher percentage increases for rural households), and (2) random overstatements (understatements) of food expenditures tend to place households in higher (lower) income groups (Bouis and Haddad 1992; Bouis 1994). The effect of this second factor, however, is reduced by the use of fitted per capita expenditure quintiles.

Table 7.6—Food expenditure and calorie shares, by cereals, nonstaple plant foods, and animal/fish products, by region, 1997

	Food expenditures by region				
	Metropolitan	Lower urban	Lower rural	Upper urban	Upper rural
			(percent)		
Budget shares					
Cereals	13	17	21	13	21
Nonstaple plant foods	39	41	39	41	40
Animal and fish products	47	42	40	46	39
Food expenditures in the highest income quintile over lowest income quintile			(ratio)		
All foods	2.69	2.07	2.02	2.65	2.62
Cereals	1.45	1.20	1.62	1.56	1.45
Nonstaple plant foods	2.48	2.17	2.42	2.74	2.55
Animal and fish products	3.52	2.50	1.94	3.02	3.79
	Calorie availability by region				
			(percent)		
Calorie shares					
Cereals	48	53	56	47	58
Nonstaple plant foods	36	35	32	39	32
Animal and fish products	16	12	12	14	10
Calorie availability in the highest income quintile over lowest income quintile			(ratio)		
All foods	1.50	1.42	1.72	1.46	1.66
Cereals	1.10	1.10	1.55	1.07	1.34
Nonstaple plant foods	1.73	1.81	1.97	1.68	2.08
Animal and fish products	2.90	2.10	1.97	2.78	2.99

Sources: Tables 7.1–7.5.

That more expensive sources of calories are purchased as incomes rise is demonstrated in a different form in the bottom sections of Tables 7.1 to 7.5, which show calories purchased per 10 piasters. In all regions, cereals are the least expensive source of calories, followed by sugar and sweets, oil, and pulses, which are roughly twice as expensive as cereals as sources of energy. With the exception of beverages, which contribute a negligible amount of calories to the diet, meat (which includes fish) is the most expensive source of calories in all regions, from 14 to 19 times as expensive as cereals, depending on region. Eggs and milk are 5 to 7 times as expensive as cereals as a source of energy, depending on region. In all regions, the cost of vegetables and fruits as sources of calories is higher than eggs and milk but lower than meat.

Patterns of Consumption for Disaggregate Cereals

Table 7.7 shows monthly per capita quantity of cereal consumption (in grams) by type of cereals and by region. In the three urban regions, consumption of four cereals is significant: subsidized *baladi* bread, all other breads, rice, and macaroni. Depending on the region, subsidized *baladi* bread accounts for 44–56 percent of total cereal consumption; rice, 14–26 percent; other breads, 6–15 percent; and macaroni, 6–7 percent.

In the two rural regions, cereal consumption is more diversified. In addition to the four cereal products just discussed, which are predominant in urban areas, consumption of four additional cereal products are also significant: subsidized wheat flour, wheat flour from the free market, wheat, and maize flour. In the rural Lower and Upper Egypt regions, respectively, subsidized *baladi* bread accounts for 25 and 23 percent of cereal consumption; subsidized *baladi* wheat flour, 6 and 21 percent; rice, 28 and 7 percent; wheat, 14 and 15 percent; free-market wheat flour, 5 and 13 percent; maize flour, 12 and 13 percent; macaroni, 5 and 3 percent; and other breads, 4 and 3 percent. Subsidized and free-market wheat flour are more important in Upper Egypt and rice is more important in Lower Egypt. Otherwise the percentage shares are quite similar between rural areas in Lower and Upper Egypt.

Food Demand Parameter Estimates

Demand parameter estimates are essential tools used in predicting outcomes of various policy reforms and in undertaking projections of food demand. For example, if the price of rice in the Egyptian domestic markets falls due to the reduction of the import tariff on rice, how much more rice will likely be consumed by people in different regions? What will be the effect on market demand for bread, pulses, cooking oil, or meat? If the price of subsidized *baladi* bread is increased, how will the de-

Table 7.7—Regional patterns of cereal consumption

Food item	Metropolitan	Lower urban	Lower rural	Upper urban	Upper rural
	(per capita consumption per month in grams)				
Total cereals	14,084	16,201	17,057	14,849	17,835
Subsidized *baladi* bread (flour equivalent)	7,912	8,339	4,328	6,509	4,049
Wheat flour (subsidized)	0	325	988	1,407	3,697
Wheat flour (free market)	307	519	908	606	2,253
All other breads (flour equivalent)	2,003	939	643	2,183	507
Wheat	57	390	2,379	379	2,698
Rice	2,570	4,141	4,735	2,111	1,317
Macaroni	1,017	1,033	768	1,004	600
Maize flour	62	351	2,018	435	2,237
Other cereals	156	164	290	215	477

Source: IFPRI Food Security Research Project in Egypt, "Egypt Integrated Household Survey, 1997."

mand of rich and poor consumers change for *baladi* bread and other food items? If per capita income rises while domestic sugar production remains static, how much sugar will have to be imported to keep prices stable? Estimates of income, own-price, and cross-price elasticities of demand are needed to answer such questions.

A number of studies in Egypt provide price and income elasticities for various commodities. A complete demand matrix was estimated by von Braun (1981) using the Linear Expenditure System (LES), based on data from three household expenditure surveys of 1958/59, 1964/65, and 1974/75, conducted by CAPMAS. Alderman and von Braun (1984) estimated a complete demand system in order to study the effects of the Egyptian food subsidy system, based on IFPRI's 1982 household expenditure survey data. A more recent work by Fayyad, Johnson, and El Kishin (1995) provides estimates of a complete demand system, using time series data for the period 1981 to 1992. However, a major drawback of this study is that the estimated parameters are subject to an identification problem because time series data were used.

A number of studies estimated price and income elasticities for some selected commodities. These studies include the work of Shalaby (1978), Mesilhy (1980), and Ali (1991). Three other studies provide only income or expenditure elasticity estimates: Ibrahim (1988); Ayaad (1994); and Ali and Adams (1996).

The estimates of demand parameters in Egypt in the present study differ from the previous studies mainly in two respects. First, the parameter estimates are based on the most recent primary data from the 1997 EIHS, which was a nationally representative household survey conducted by IFPRI. Second, for the first time in Egypt, this study estimates demand elasticities for each of the five regions of the country.

Estimation Method and Data Requirements

In this report, demand parameters have been estimated using a relatively new method, labeled the Food Characteristic Demand System (FCDS). It is based on the 1997 EIHS data.[35] The methodology and data requirements for estimation of the FCDS are discussed in detail in Bouis (1996). According to the FCDS, a household's food acquisition behavior is motivated by (1) demand for energy (calories) to alleviate hunger; (2) demand for variety in the diet; (3) demand for food-group specific tastes; and (4) demand for tastes inherent in particular foods. By specifying utility as an explicit function of these four characteristics, a complete matrix of own- and cross-price elasticities can be derived for *n* foods and one nonfood from the prior specification of a minimum of four elasticities (or some combination of food elasticities and/or utility function parameters), while avoiding any assumption of separability between foods. Appendix D provides the mathematical formulation of the FCDS.

Estimation of the FCDS parameters requires data on (1) per capita quantities of food for each food group; (2) prices paid per kilogram for each food group; (3) calo-

[35] An attempt has been made by IFPRI researchers to estimate food demand parameters econometrically through use of the Almost Ideal Demand System (AIDS), using the 1997 EIHS data. However, plausible estimates of demand parameters could not be derived for a number of commodities, mainly because of the lack of variation in prices of commodities from the single round of cross-section EIHS data.

rie conversion rates per kilogram for each food group; (4) total nonfood expenditure; and (5) the ratio of adult equivalents to total household members. The 1997 EIHS provides data to meet all of these requirements except calorie conversion rates. In this study, the quantity of food acquired by a household was converted to calories using Egyptian food composition tables (FAO 1982).

Results and Their Interpretation

A summary of expenditure and own-price elasticities is presented in Tables 7.8 and 7.9, respectively. The own-price and expenditure elasticities are provided for 16 food groups and 1 nonfood group. These elasticities are disaggregated by five regions (Metropolitan, urban Lower Egypt, rural Lower Egypt, urban Upper Egypt, and rural Upper Egypt), by all urban and all rural, and by all Egypt. The elasticities are also disaggregated into urban poor and nonpoor and rural poor and nonpoor groups (Table 7.10).

How Does Income Affect Consumption Patterns?

Table 7.8 presents the expenditure elasticities of all commodity groups by regions. Note that the expenditure elasticities for subsidized *baladi* bread and subsidized wheat flour are marginally negative in all regions of Egypt. This indicates that subsidized *baladi* bread and subsidized wheat flour are marginally "inferior" goods (as opposed to "normal" goods, such as rice or meat) in Egypt. In other words, as household expenditures increase by 10 percent, demand for subsidized *baladi* bread will fall by 1.5 percent in urban areas, and demand for subsidized wheat flour will fall by 1.2 percent in rural areas. Since the consumption levels of wheat and maize flour are quite low in urban Egypt, demand elasticities (both expenditure and price elasticities) have not been computed separately for these food items for urban areas, but they are incorporated in the "other cereals" group.

How Responsive Are Demands to Changes in Prices?

Table 7.9 presents the own-price elasticities of all commodity groups by regions.[36] The estimates suggest that, except for subsidized *baladi* bread, Egyptian households in general are highly responsive to changes in food prices. If, for example, the price of subsidized *baladi* bread is increased by 10 percent, consumers living in the metropolitan governorates would decrease their demand for subsidized *baladi* bread by 2.8 percent. However, if the price of meat increases by 10 percent, demand for meat by Egyptian consumers in all regions would decrease by 10 percent, because meat has a unitary own-price elasticity in all regions.

Note that price elasticities have not been estimated separately for rationed sugar and rationed cooking oil distributed through the *tamween* shops at subsidized prices,

[36] Estimates of the cross-price elasticities are not presented in this report. See Bouis, Ahmed, and Hamza (1999) for estimates of the cross-price elasticities from the 1997 EIHS, and their interpretation.

Table 7.8—Expenditure elasticities of all commodity groups, by region

Commodities	Metropolitan	Lower urban	Lower rural	Upper urban	Upper rural	All urban	All rural	Egypt
Subsidized *baladi* bread	–0.15	–0.12	–0.11	–0.18	–0.07	–0.15	–0.10	–0.11
Subsidized wheat flour	. . .	. . .	–0.08	. . .	–0.14	. . .	–0.12	–0.09
Unsubsidized wheat flour	. . .	. . .	0.18	. . .	0.07	. . .	0.12	0.19
Fino bread	0.24	0.20	0.08	0.18	0.11	0.22	0.09	0.13
Rice	0.23	0.21	0.23	0.22	0.33	0.22	0.27	0.24
Maize flour	. . .	. . .	–0.02	. . .	0.13	. . .	0.03	0.02
Other cereals	0.34	0.30	0.29	0.26	0.48	0.31	0.38	0.37
Cooking oil	0.23	0.22	0.26	0.19	0.28	0.21	0.26	0.23
Sugar	0.50	0.56	0.62	0.53	0.59	0.52	0.61	0.56
Pulses	0.45	0.46	0.51	0.43	0.55	0.45	0.53	0.48
Vegetables	0.58	0.61	0.66	0.59	0.70	0.59	0.68	0.63
Fruits	0.58	0.61	0.65	0.59	0.66	0.59	0.66	0.62
Meat	0.65	0.71	0.78	0.68	0.83	0.68	0.81	0.73
Eggs and milk	0.59	0.60	0.65	0.59	0.67	0.59	0.66	0.62
Condiments	0.60	0.66	0.72	0.63	0.75	0.63	0.74	0.67
Beverages	0.69	0.75	0.84	0.72	0.87	0.72	0.86	0.78
Nonfoods	1.48	1.61	1.79	1.55	1.87	1.54	1.83	1.66

Source: Computed by the authors, based on data from IFPRI Food Security Research Project in Egypt, "Egypt Integrated Household Survey, 1997."
Note: Ellipsis (. . .) indicates a nil or negligible amount.

Table 7.9—Uncompensated (observed) own-price elasticities of demand for all commodity groups, by region

Commodities	Metropolitan	Lower urban	Lower rural	Upper urban	Upper rural	All urban	All rural	Egypt
Subsidized *baladi* bread	–0.28	–0.24	–0.37	–0.29	–0.51	–0.27	–0.44	–0.33
Subsidized wheat flour	. . .	. . .	–0.74	. . .	–0.56	. . .	–0.65	–0.78
Unsubsidized wheat flour	. . .	. . .	–0.91	. . .	–0.84	. . .	–0.88	–0.92
Fino bread	–0.86	–0.86	–0.91	–0.81	–0.90	–0.85	–0.90	–0.90
Rice	–0.87	–0.82	–0.83	–0.87	–0.91	–0.86	–0.87	–0.87
Maize flour	. . .	. . .	–0.85	. . .	–0.86	. . .	–0.85	–0.88
Other cereals	–0.91	–0.87	–0.87	–0.83	–0.91	–0.88	–0.89	–0.91
Cooking oil	–0.87	–0.85	–0.89	–0.84	–0.89	–0.86	–0.89	–0.89
Sugar	–0.96	–0.97	–0.98	–0.96	–0.96	–0.96	–0.98	–0.98
Pulses	–0.94	–0.93	–0.95	–0.92	–0.94	–0.93	–0.94	–0.95
Vegetables	–0.98	–0.97	–0.97	–0.98	–0.98	–0.97	–0.97	–0.98
Fruits	–0.99	–0.99	–1.00	–0.99	–1.00	–0.99	–1.00	–1.00
Meat	–1.00	–1.00	–1.00	–1.00	–1.01	– 1.00	–1.01	–1.00
Eggs and milk	–0.98	–0.98	–0.99	–0.98	–0.99	–0.98	–0.99	–0.99
Condiments	–1.00	–1.00	–1.00	–1.00	–1.01	–1.00	–1.01	–1.01
Beverages	–1.00	–1.00	–1.00	–1.00	–1.00	–1.00	–1.00	–1.00
Nonfoods	–1.30	–1.34	–1.39	–1.33	–1.44	–1.32	–1.42	–1.37

Source: Computed by authors based on data from IFPRI Food Security Research Project in Egypt, "Egypt Integrated Household Survey, 1997."
Note: Ellipsis (. . .) indicates a nil or negligible amount.

Table 7.10—Own-price and expenditure elasticities for the lowest 40 percent (poor) and highest 60 percent (nonpoor) of income distribution

	Own-price elasticities				Expenditure elasticities			
	All urban		All rural		All urban		All rural	
Food item	**Poor**	**Nonpoor**	**Poor**	**Nonpoor**	**Poor**	**Nonpoor**	**Poor**	**Nonpoor**
Subsidized *baladi* bread	–0.25	–0.28	–0.50	–0.41	–0.11	–0.17	–0.09	–0.09
Subsidized wheat flour	. . .	. . .	–0.69	–0.65	. . .	. . .	–0.10	–0.11
Unsubsidized wheat flour	. . .	. . .	–0.91	–0.87	. . .	. . .	0.16	0.14
Fino bread	–0.91	–0.81	–0.96	–0.88	0.30	0.18	0.16	0.08
Rice	–0.89	–0.84	–0.92	–0.85	0.32	0.17	0.40	0.23
Maize flour	. . .	. . .	–0.89	–0.84	. . .	. . .	0.08	0.05
Other cereals	–0.89	–0.87	–0.93	–0.87	0.38	0.27	0.50	0.35
Cooking oil	–0.90	–0.83	–0.95	–0.87	0.30	0.17	0.37	0.24
Sugar	–0.99	–0.95	–1.00	–0.96	0.60	0.48	0.72	0.56
Pulses	–0.95	–0.93	–0.97	–0.93	0.54	0.40	0.65	0.48
Vegetables	–0.98	–0.97	–0.98	–0.97	0.65	0.56	0.75	0.64
Fruits	–1.01	–0.99	–1.03	–0.99	0.64	0.56	0.71	0.63
Meat	–1.01	–0.99	–1.01	–1.00	0.77	0.63	0.92	0.75
Eggs and milk	–1.00	–0.97	–1.01	–0.98	0.66	0.55	0.77	0.61
Condiments	–1.01	–1.00	–1.02	– 1.00	0.71	0.58	0.83	0.68
Beverages	–1.00	–1.00	–1.00	–1.00	0.81	0.67	0.97	0.79
Nonfoods	–1.42	–1.26	–1.53	–1.36	1.72	1.43	2.07	1.69

Source: Computed by the authors based on data from IFPRI Food Security Research Project in Egypt, "Egypt Integrated Household Survey, 1997."
Note: Ellipsis (. . .) indicates a nil or negligible amount.

because the EIHS data suggest that rationed sugar and cooking oil are inframarginal for the Egyptian consumers. Therefore, as explained in Chapter 5, any change in ration prices of subsidized sugar and oil would not affect household budget allocation except through a (relatively small) income effect. For this reason, sugar and oil are treated as aggregate goods in estimating their price elasticities.

Demand Elasticities for Poor and Nonpoor Consumers

Table 7.10 presents the estimates of own-price and expenditure elasticities for urban and rural Egypt, disaggregated by poor and nonpoor households. In this analysis, the lowest 40 percent of income distribution of the population is considered poor, while the top 60 percent of the population is considered nonpoor.

The estimates of own-price elasticities suggest that, in general, poor households are more price responsive than nonpoor households. Expenditure elasticities are also substantially higher for the poor than for the nonpoor, which is a common pattern.

Subsidized *baladi* bread is an inferior good for both poor and nonpoor households in urban and rural Egypt, as the negative expenditure elasticities indicate. If, for example, per capita income of the poor in urban areas increases by 10 percent, then their demand for subsidized *baladi* bread would decrease by 1.1 percent. Also, subsidized wheat flour is an inferior good for both poor and nonpoor households in rural areas. More expensive food items (such as meat, fruit, vegetables, eggs, and milk) have relatively high expenditure elasticities for both poor and nonpoor households.

Summary

Subsidized *baladi* bread and wheat flour contribute importantly to total calorie intakes. However, the impact of the food subsidy system on the overall dietary pattern is primarily through its modest effect on household income. That is, if all subsidies were removed, bread consumption would surely decline because of the higher price, but this would be compensated for by increases in consumption of other food staples such as rice, macaroni, and maize flour to maintain rather high levels of calorie intake. Consumers reveal a strong preference for consumption of nonstaple foods, particularly animal products, so that the primary effect of a decline in income caused by removal of food subsidies would be reduced dietary quality, that is a modest decline in consumption of animal products and other nonstaple foods.

According to the food demand matrixes of price and income elasticities developed for low- and high-income groups and for urban and rural areas in Egypt, subsidized *baladi* bread and wheat flour are slightly inferior goods for both poor and nonpoor households, as the negative expenditure elasticities (but low absolute values) indicate. If all food subsidies were to be removed, bread consumption would decline, but rather high levels of calorie intake would continue to be maintained as a result of increases in consumption of other staples.

CHAPTER 8

Policy Options and Their Simulated General Equilibrium Effects

It is clear from government documents, interviews with government officials, and MOTS statements, that the government has no intention of dismantling the food subsidy system because of its social and political importance. It is widely agreed, however, that there is significant scope for reforming the existing system in ways that enhance its efficiency and effectiveness in reaching the poor. This chapter describes and evaluates the simulated effects of a number of possible policy options to reduce leakage, to better target the poor, and to improve the cost-effectiveness of the food subsidy system. These policy options emerge from the analysis presented in this study, as well as ideas generated by formal interviews with policymakers and stakeholders, and direct day-to-day contact with government officials and Egyptian researchers as part of the collaborative project conducted by IFPRI in Egypt during the 1996–99 period.[37]

A Computable General Equilibrium (CGE) model is used to explore the short-run equilibrium effects of a set of alternative options for the operation of Egypt's food subsidy system. The economywide perspective of the analysis makes it possible to consider the broader economic repercussions of different policy options. The analysis highlights not only the effects of policies on the micro level (for example, changes in household welfare), but also on the macro level (for example, on the government budget) as well as the trade-offs involved.

The Egypt Food CGE Model

The simulation analysis of this chapter is based on a CGE model of Egypt. CGE models may be defined as economywide models, the solutions to which depict a simulta-

[37] All research efforts of the IFPRI Food Security Research Project in Egypt were made in collaboration with Egyptian researchers and policymakers from various academic and government institutions. The Egyptian collaborators helped inform IFPRI's research, making it relevant to the needs of Egypt.

neous general equilibrium in all markets of the economy. They are widely applied to policy analysis in developing countries and have a comparative advantage in the analysis of tax and subsidy policies, in particular when there is a need to consider links between different producing sectors, links between macro and micro levels, and the disaggregated impact of changes in policies and exogenous shocks on sectoral structure, household welfare, and income distribution. CGE analyses of the Egyptian economy have a relatively long history, with the first model dating back to 1976.[38]

The CGE model of Egypt used here, called the Food CGE Model, is based on an earlier model of Egypt (Löfgren and Kherallah 1998).[39] It is structured in the tradition of trade-focused CGE models of developing countries described in Dervis, de Melo, and Robinson (1982). The distinguishing features of the current model include a detailed treatment of households, agriculture, and food processing, as well as food subsidies and the benefits they provide to households. Table 8.1 shows the disaggregation of institutions, factors, and activities in the model.

In most sectors, producers maximize profits subject to production functions with neoclassical substitutability for factors and fixed coefficients for intermediate inputs. In agriculture, the model captures major agronomic area constraints and links between crop and livestock production (for example, the use of manure as an input in crop production). Households receive the bulk of their incomes from the factors they control, including worker remittances from abroad, and they use their income to save and consume (according to demand functions derived from utility maximization). The government receives tax and transfer revenues, which it uses for consumption spending and subsidies. Subsidized bread and flour are available to consumers at fixed prices in nonrationed quantities. Given that subsidized oil and sugar are rationed and, for most households, supplemented by market purchases, the subsidy on other foods has little direct impact on the quantities consumed of these two commodities. Hence, the subsidy on oil and sugar is treated as a cash transfer from the government to the households. The subsidy treatment also considers that, as the result of leakages, part of the subsidy does not reach the households through the intended channels.

Flexible prices clear most commodity and factor markets. With the primary exception of grains (which are perfect substitutes), outputs that are sold domestically and traded internationally are imperfect substitutes. The macro rules of the model determine how balance is achieved for the accounts of the government, the rest of the world (the current account of the balance of payments), and savings and investment. For the government account, a change in the direct tax rate (the change in the rate is uniform across all households) ensures that government savings are maintained at the initial level.[40] In the balance of the rest of the world, foreign savings

[38] See Löfgren (1994b) for a survey of CGE models of Egypt.

[39] The analysis in Löfgren and Kherallah (1998), which is incorporated into Kherallah et al. (2000), is focused on Egypt's wheat sector, including the impact of fluctuations in international wheat prices on wheat production and the food subsidy system.

[40] For example, if there is a need to reduce direct tax rates, and the initial tax rates of two different household types are 10 percent and 4 percent, they may decline to 9 percent and 3 percent, respectively.

Table 8.1—Disaggregation of factors, institutions, and activities in the CGE model

Set	Elements	Description
Institutions (12)	Households	Rural and urban, both disaggregated by quintile
	Government	
	Rest of the world	
Factors of production (5)	Capital	Agricultural and nonagricultural
	Labor	Agricultural and nonagricultural
	Water	
	Summer land	
	Winter land	
Activities (28)	Winter crops	Wheat, legumes, long berseem, short berseem, winter vegetables, other winter crops
	Summer crops	Cotton, rice, maize (including sorghum), summer vegetables, other summer crops
	Perennial crops	Fruits, sugarcane
	Other agriculture and food processing	Animal agriculture, subsidized bread, unsubsidized bread, subsidized flour, unsubsidized flour, other food processing
	Other	Oil, cotton ginning, textiles, other industry, electricity, construction, government services, transportation, other services

(the current account deficit) is similarly fixed; the exchange rate is the equilibrating variable. On the spending side of the savings-investment balance, aggregate investment is fixed in quantity terms. On the savings side, uniform changes in the savings rates of each household category are used to generate the level of total savings needed to finance aggregate investment.

The model, which is solved in a comparative static mode, provides a simulation laboratory for doing controlled experiments, changing policies and other exogenous conditions, and measuring the impact of these changes. Each solution provides a full set of economic indicators, including household incomes; prices, supplies and demands for factors and commodities (including foreign trade for the latter); and macroeconomic data.

Appendix E provides a more detailed description of the CGE model and its database. Tables E.1 to E.6 in Appendix E include additional data and simulation results as well as a mathematical statement of the CGE model.

Policy Options and Their Simulated Effects

Before presenting the policy options, it is important to emphasize that in assessing these options, the government will have to take into account the political and administrative feasibility as well as the economic costs and benefits. Therefore, the following policy options are motivated by and assessed from economic, administrative, and political perspectives.

Among the seven policy options presented, the first five options were simulated with the CGE model. The remaining two options, which involve geographic targeting to specific urban neighborhoods (Option 6) and to specific governorates (Option 7), could not be simulated, since the CGE model is a national model. The simulations are defined in Table 8.2 and their results are summarized in Table 8.3. Unless otherwise noted, the simulations are based on the assumption that the government uses the savings that result from the changes in subsidy policy to reduce direct taxes (with the same decline in the tax rate for all households).

The policy options in focus here are those that would strengthen the targeting of the food subsidies to the poor without adding to government costs. The options vary in terms of their perceived political feasibility. While it is difficult to precisely rank options in terms of political feasibility, there is a widespread perception in Egypt that policy reforms affecting the price of subsidized *baladi* bread are the most politically sensitive. Ultimately, policymakers considering what action to take on the issue of food subsidy reform (in Egypt and elsewhere) can combine different options to produce an outcome that meets their political, economic, and social goals. The choice of options also depends on how goals are prioritized: if political feasibility is the primary goal, the ranking of options may be different than if cost savings are the primary goal. Expansion of the social safety net, in turn, may also point toward options that result in higher costs. Table 8.4 highlights the strengths, weaknesses, and other salient features of these options.

Option 1: Target Rationed Cooking Oil and Sugar Subsidies to Needy Households

Since 1981, there have been two categories of ration cards for subsidized cooking oil and sugar: the green card, which has a higher rate of subsidy and is intended for low-income families, and the red card, which has a lower rate of subsidy and is intended for people in higher-income occupations. However, the current ration-card subsidy system is very loosely targeted. This study estimates that two-thirds of card-holding households in the top three expenditure quintiles, who may be considered nonpoor, hold the higher-subsidy green ration cards and only one-third hold red cards. Sixty-one percent of all green cards belong to households in the three richest quintiles, and these households receive 62 percent of the total rationed subsidy benefits. In contrast, 10 percent of the households in the poorest two quintiles hold red cards, although they should appropriately hold the higher-subsidy green ration cards. This report also found that about 14 percent of the Egyptian households in the poorest two quintiles do not hold ration cards.

A two-phase policy reform might first seek to transfer nonpoor consumers from the green card to the red card and poor consumers from the red card to the green card. It would also bring the poor who currently do not hold any ration card into the green card system. This would demonstrate the government's desire to provide a ration-

Table 8.2—Simulation assumptions

Item	Simulations							
	Targeting oil/sugar subsidy + income tax cut (1)	Wheat-maize flour + income tax cut (2a)	Wheat-maize flour + income tax cut + leakage cut (2b)	Wheat-maize flour + income tax cut + leakage cut + yield increase (2c)	Eliminating oil/sugar subsidy + income tax cut (3)	Targeting total food subsidy + income tax cut (4)	Eliminating total food subsidy + income tax cut (5a)	Eliminating total food subsidy + transfer to needy (5b)
	(percentage change)							
Oil and sugar subsidy to nonneedy	−100				−100	−100	−100	−100
Bread and flour subsidy to nonneedy						−100	−100	−100
Oil and sugar subsidy to needy					−100		−100	−100
Bread and flour subsidy to needy					−100	−100		
Leakage for oil and sugar subsidy	−62				−100	−62	−100	−100
Leakage for bread and flour subsidy			−100	−100		−60	−100	−100
Government savings to income tax cut?	YES	YES	YES	YES	YES	YES	YES	
Government savings to cash transfer to needy?								YES
Maize flour (20 percent) in subsidized flour?		YES	YES	YES				
Maize yield increase and fixed maize area?				YES				

card safety net to the poor people who have slipped through the system, which should enhance the overall political feasibility of food subsidy reform. Moreover, conversion of red cards to green cards for those poor families who currently hold red cards would reflect government efforts to provide a higher level of food subsidy benefits to the poor, which should mitigate public criticism that this reform simply sought to reduce subsidy costs by transferring people from the green card to the red card.

Targeting the green cards to the poor and the red cards to the nonpoor would require identification of both poor and nonpoor households, something that is not always easy. To effectively implement a targeted program, it would be necessary to rely on a method such as proxy means testing. Capacity-strengthening activities would also be needed for the government administrators who would run the program.[41]

In the second phase, the red card subsidy may be removed by raising the ration prices of sugar and oil to their market price levels. In the event that the price subsidy were completely removed for red card holders, the red card would still function as an entitlement to a quantity ration in the event of a future emergency.

Simulated Effects (Simulation 1). In the first simulation, oil and sugar subsidies (representing 23 percent of total food subsidy spending) are targeted to the needy, defined as the bottom two quintiles (40 percent) of the population in both rural and urban areas,[42] while eliminating these subsidies for the top three quintiles. The latter groups continue to have access to these commodities but at full market prices. It is assumed that the oil-sugar subsidy leakage declines in proportion to the reduction in subsidy spending. IFPRI research shows that targeting can be achieved at a minimal cost, in particular since current staff at MOTS could manage the targeting without any need for new hiring.[43]

In economic terms, given that the ration card subsidy is treated as inframarginal (that is, it is nondistorting, having no direct impact on the quantities consumed of oil and sugar), the subsidy cut is equivalent to a withdrawal of cash benefits from nonneedy ration card holders. In addition, a cash benefit is withdrawn from those who benefited from the subsidy leakage.

The results are summarized in Table 8.3. The reductions in oil and sugar subsidies are about 62 percent and the reductions in overall food subsidy spending are about 14 percent. This spending cut permits the government to reduce income tax collection by 3.5 percent (via a uniform cut in the income tax rate for all households), while keep-

[41] Proxy means testing is a relatively new and low cost approach that seeks to identify indicators of household income. It uses regression equations to determine the strength of association between indicators and household incomes. IFPRI has developed a proxy means testing method of determining eligibility for ration card food subsidies in Egypt (Ahmed and Bouis 1998; Ahmed et al. 1999).

[42] For an applied analysis of subsidy targeting in Egypt, see Ahmed et al. (1999). They analyze the use of a proxy means test to determine eligibility for food subsidies, an approach that appears to be preferable to targeting on the basis of income information.

[43] According to IFPRI estimates, the one-time cost of training and materials needed for targeting is around LE 14 million, an insignificant amount corresponding to 0.4 percent of the total annual food subsidy budget (or 0.005 percent of GDP).

Table 8.3—Summary of simulation results

Item	Base[a]	Simulations							
		Targeting oil/sugar subsidy + income tax cut (1)	Wheat-maize flour + income tax cut (2a)	Wheat-maize flour + income tax cut + leakage cut (2b)	Wheat-maize flour + income tax cut + leakage cut + yield increase (2c)	Eliminating oil/sugar subsidy + income tax cut (3)	Targeting total food subsidy + income tax cut (4)	Eliminating total food subsidy + income tax cut (5a)	Eliminating total food subsidy + transfer to needy (5b)
	(million LE)	(percentage change from base)							
Real per capita household consumption (LE at 1996/97 prices)									
Rural households	2,459.1	0.0	0.1	0.1	0.5	0.0	0.4	0.6	1.2
(by quintile)									
1	1,269.3	0.2	0.1	0.2	0.7	−0.3	0.9	−0.7	7.4
2	1,670.2	0.2	0.1	0.1	0.7	−0.2	0.8	−0.2	5.6
3	2,130.9	−0.2	0.1	0.2	0.5	−0.1	−0.2	0.5	−0.8
4	2,672.1	−0.1	0.1	0.1	0.5	0.0	0.0	0.7	−0.8
5	4,552.9	0.0	0.1	0.1	0.4	0.1	0.5	1.2	−0.1
Urban households	4,326.3	0.0	−0.1	−0.1	0.3	0.0	−0.1	−0.2	−0.7
(by quintile)									
1	1,713.5	0.2	−0.2	−0.1	0.5	−0.2	0.1	−2.3	2.8
2	2,456.5	0.2	−0.1	−0.1	0.5	−0.1	0.2	−1.4	1.7
3	3,361.2	−0.1	−0.1	−0.1	0.4	0.0	−0.8	−0.6	−2.4

4	4,647.0	–0.1	–0.1	–0.1	0.3	0.1	–0.5	–0.2	–2.0
5	9,453.2	0.0	0.0	–0.1	0.2	0.1	0.3	0.7	–0.8
Needy households	1,734.1	0.2	0.0	0.0	0.6	–0.2	0.5	–1.1	4.2
Nonneedy households	4,279.7	0.0	0.0	0.0	0.3	0.1	0.0	0.5	–1.0
Average household	3,261.5	0.0	0.0	0.0	0.4	0.0	0.1	0.2	0.1
Government budget items (million LE at 1996/97 prices)									
Spending on food subsidies	3,741.6	–14.4	–5.9	–17.4	–19.5	–23.4	–64.2	–100.0	100.0
Spending on bread and flour subsidies	2,867.0	0.0	–7.7	–22.75	–25.5	0.0	–64.9	–100.0	–100.0
Spending on oil and sugar subsidies	874.6	–61.6	0.0	0.0	0.0	–100.0	–61.6	–100.0	–100.0
Income tax revenue	14,591.0	–3.5	–1.3	–4.0	–3.9	–5.7	–16.4	–25.4	–1.0
Cash transfers to needy[a]									3,642.5
Food and agriculture trade (billion $)									
Net imports	1,962.8	0.0	–6.0	–6.0	–10.9	0.0	–1.8	–1.2	–0.4
Wheat and flour imports	1,100.4	0.0	–12.7	–12.7	–19.8	0.0	–6.9	–7.1	–5.9
Exchange rate (LE per unit of foreign currency)	1.0	0.0	–0.3	–0.3	–0.5	0.0	–0.6	–1.4	–1.2
Maize yield (normalized to 1 for Base)	1.0		0.1	0.1	11.4				
Maize area (million feddans)	2.0		11.6	11.6	0.0				

Note: Values smaller than ± 0.1 are shown as 0.0.

[a] Data in columns 1–5b show percentage change from figures in base column.

Table 8.4—Comparison of policy options for food subsidy reform

Option Number	Option description	Pros	Cons	Tried before?	Political acceptability	Administrative feasibility	Other issues
1	Target rationed cooking oil and sugar subsidies						
	a. Transfer nonpoor consumers from green to red card and poor consumers from red to green card, and bring the poor without cards into the green card system	Better targets subsidy to poor; cost savings, captures some of poorer people who do not receive subsidy; increases equity in the system	None	Yes	High; shows government concern for subsidies as safety net; may cushion political impact on other measures	Depends on level of government effort to target using proxy means tests	How many to move; how to administer; whether to publicize
	b. Then, in a second phase, remove subsidy on the red card	Better targets remaining subsidy; cost savings	Politically sensitive?	No	Medium	Should be no problem	Level of price increase; timing of policy change; how to publicize
2	Mix maize flour with subsidized wheat flour at four mills	Reduces leakage at bakery and warehouse levels; decreases wheat imports; cost savings	Currently limited scope for higher maize procurement from domestic production	Yes, to limited degree	High	Proven	Requires more maize procurement from domestic production or imports; needs research on farmers' maize marketing decisions
3	Eliminate sugar and cooking oil subsidies	23 percent savings in total food subsidy costs	May hurt poorer card holders	No	Medium	Easy	Timing; how to publicize

4	Target all food subsidies to needy households	64 percent savings in total food subsidy costs; the needy gain; helps wheat market to function more efficiently	Politically unrealistic at present	No	Low/medium	Difficult	Many; timing; identifying poor; distributing coupons; how to publicize, etc.
5	Eliminate all food subsidies	Cost savings	Will hurt the poor; politically unrealistic	No	Low	Easy	Timing; whether and how to compensate the poor
6	Target *baladi* bread subsidies to poor neighborhoods in urban areas	Better targets subsidy; cost savings	Politically sensitive?	Yes	Medium	Easy, once boundaries are determined	How to determine where the boundaries are between poor and wealthy neighborhoods
7	Reallocate subsidized food supply among governorates using poverty levels as a criteria	Better targets to poor; can improve government popularity in areas that see increase in benefits		No		Depends on capacity of areas to receive higher benefits	Whether to add benefits or reallocate benefits; how to increase capacity where it is weak
	a. Add new benefits for governorates where benefits are much lower than poverty rates		Fiscal cost		High		
	b. Reallocate benefits for governorates where benefits are much higher than poverty rates for those where they are much lower		Politically sensitive		Medium/low		

ing government savings constant.[44] Given that the subsidy is nondistorting, there is no efficiency gain: aggregate household consumption does not change.[45] In both urban and rural regions, the two bottom quintiles enjoy small gains (since they receive the tax cut without any subsidy withdrawal). The third and fourth quintiles lose slightly (the tax cut does not fully compensate for the subsidy loss), whereas the top quintile is unaffected (the tax cut and the subsidy loss are of equivalent cash value).

Option 2: Mix Maize Flour with Subsidized Wheat Flour at Flour Mills

A tactic for reducing and preventing leakages of subsidized wheat flour is to mix maize flour with subsidized 82 percent-extraction wheat flour at flour mills and then to supply the mixed flour to both *baladi* bread bakeries and warehouses. This would prevent leakage of subsidized flour before it reaches consumers, because the mixed flour cannot be sifted into higher-quality 72 percent-extraction wheat flour for eventual sale on the open market at a higher price. Estimates in this report show that, in 1997, the total cost of leakage from subsidized wheat flour supplied to bakeries and warehouses amounted to about LE 428 million (US$126 million). The government incurred this cost, while the benefits accrued not to the intended consumers but to those who misappropriated the subsidy.

The strategy of mixing maize flour with wheat flour had already been implemented in selected bakeries on an experimental basis starting in late 1996. This experiment has since been extended to subsidized flour sold to consumers through warehouses. The government's main objective in this initiative is to decrease the wheat import bill and the cost of subsidizing bread and flour consumption (maize flour is cheaper since maize grain costs less and has a higher extraction rate).

A field investigation conducted by the IFPRI project staff in Egypt discovered that maize flour and 82 percent-extraction wheat flour were supplied in separate sacks to bakeries and warehouses, rather than packaged in mixed form. This practice of supplying maize and wheat flour in separate sacks does not prevent leakage because subsidized 82 percent-extraction wheat flour can still be sifted down to 72 percent-extraction wheat flour. Therefore, in order to reduce leakage, it is essential that MOTS mixes maize flour with wheat flour *at flour mills,* and then distributes the *mixed flour* to bakeries and warehouses. This reform involves only a one-time cost of reconfiguring flour mills to mix wheat and maize flour at the mills.

A constraint to implementing this policy is that the government has so far been unable to procure sufficient domestically produced white maize to expand this initiative nationwide. Relying on imported white maize would defeat one of the main

---

[44] For the closure with fixed government savings and flexible direct tax rates, the changes in direct tax rates are equal for all household groups. For example, the tax rates may be cut by 1 percentage point for each household group, for one group from 7 percent to 6 percent and from 3 percent to 2 percent for another group.

[45] Real household consumption (at base prices) is used as the welfare indicator. Given that the population is fixed, percentage changes in total and per capita consumption are identical.

government objectives of this initiative, which is to decrease the cereal import bill. Two possible solutions are (1) to stimulate domestic maize production, and (2) to eliminate barriers that inhibit the desire of farmers to sell maize to the government. Further research is needed to understand the nature of these constraints.

Simulated Effects (Simulations 2a, 2b, and 2c). These simulations explore the impact of replacement of 100 percent wheat flour by a wheat-maize mix with a 20 percent maize share (see Table 8.3 for a summary of the results). The government uses the resulting savings to cut direct taxes. This policy is relatively broad because it introduces mixed wheat-maize flour not only for the flour used for subsidized bread but also for the subsidized flour that is sold directly to consumers. Technically, the policy shift is represented by changed input coefficients in the production of subsidized flour so that 20 percent of the wheat grain is replaced by maize. It is assumed that household demand behavior is not affected by the introduction of maize, that is, there is no significant difference in taste. A higher maize flour extraction rate (97 percent compared with 82 percent for this type of wheat flour) and a lower maize grain price (in the base year, 23 percent below the wheat price) give rise to government savings (Khalil 1999; Egypt, Ministry of Agriculture 1998).

The initial effect of the policy shift is that 20 percent of the wheat demanded for use in production of subsidized flour is shifted to maize at 65 percent of the initial cost, raising the demand for maize with a resulting increase in maize production (by almost 12 percent). This leads to reduced subsidy spending, reflecting a decline in the per-unit subsidy needed to maintain fixed prices for subsidized bread and flour. In Simulation 2a, total food subsidy spending declines by 6 percent. The resulting government savings permit a decline in direct tax collection of 1.3 percent. The shift of agricultural demand from a traded commodity (wheat) toward a nontradable one leads to a slight increase in agricultural factor incomes that, at the household level, benefits rural households. Net food imports decline substantially (by 6 percent), a reflection of resource savings (the maize flour requires fewer resources than the wheat flour for which it substitutes).

Simulation 2b looks at the impact of combining the introduction of the wheat-maize flour mix with an elimination of leakages for subsidized bread and flour. The rationale for this simulation is the difficulty of diverting mixed flour to unintended uses.

Because of the addition of the leakage cut, the decline in spending on bread and flour subsidies and the direct tax cut are almost tripled. From the perspective of saving government resources, the main benefit of the maize-wheat flour program may be that it makes leakage more difficult, not that it lowers the cost of maize flour. Incomes decline for the recipients of leaked subsidy benefits. The net impact is a small but progressive effect on income distribution. Other effects are very minor.

In Egypt, there is considerable potential for raising maize yields (Harrison 1996; Khalil 1999), possibly annulling the need to increase the maize area in the face of increased demand for white maize for use in subsidized bread and flour products. Simulation 2c poses the following questions: What is the increase in maize yields needed to avoid an increase in the maize area in the context of the shift to a wheat-maize flour mix and elimination of subsidized bread and flour leakage? What are the broader economic repercussions of such a yield change? Technically, the simulation is implemented by fixing the maize area while endogenizing maize land productivity.

As shown in Table 8.3, an 11 percent yield increase is required (very close to the relative area increase for Simulation 2b). The resulting shift in the supply curve for maize reduces the maize price, further cutting the government subsidy bill. There is an increase in agricultural and rural incomes, bringing about a multiplier process that boosts demand for agricultural products, including crops competing with maize. At the new equilibrium, consumption is higher for every household category, with the largest gains for needy households and a slightly larger aggregate gain in rural areas. However, given the income redistribution to rural households (who pay smaller income shares in direct taxes), the direct tax cut declines slightly compared with Simulation 2b. Increased productivity of land in maize production (and a return of the maize area to the base level) gives rise to changes in agricultural resource allocation, including a shift toward wheat and away from cotton and short berseem. The result is a significant decline in wheat and flour imports and an overall decline in net food and agricultural imports (by 11 percent for the latter).

Option 3: Eliminate the Sugar and Cooking Oil Subsidies

In 1997, about one-fifth of total subsidized sugar disappeared as leakage before reaching consumers, and of the remaining amount, about 62 percent went to people in the top three expenditure quintiles, who may be considered nonneedy. Analysis in Chapter 6 also suggests that, of the four subsidized foods, the rationed cooking oil subsidy is the least effective means for transferring income to consumers. Combining system leakage and targeting inefficiency, only about one-third of the total sugar and oil subsidy benefits go to the needy.

Instead of trying to improve targeting, which would likely involve additional administrative costs, the government may choose to eliminate the subsidy on rationed sugar and cooking oil.[46] As noted earlier, since purchases of subsidized sugar and cooking oil appear to be inframarginal for most households, elimination of these subsidies may be assumed to have no substitution effects, only an income effect. Income transfers from sugar and cooking oil subsidies account for only 0.7 percent and 0.4 percent, respectively, of total expenditures for the poor (bottom 40 percent of the population).

Simulated Effects (Simulation 3). In this simulation, oil and sugar subsidies (including leakage) are eliminated. After the change, the whole population pays full market prices for these commodities. In practice, this involves eliminating the ration card system (at least for its current purposes). As shown in Table 8.3, this policy re-

[46] However, these costs would most likely be small. According to IFPRI estimates, the one-time cost of training and materials needed for targeting the ration card system is merely around LE 14 million, an insignificant amount compared with other items in Egypt's food subsidy budget.

duces subsidy spending by 23 percent, while income tax revenue declines by 6 percent. Aggregate consumption does not change (since the oil and sugar subsidies are nondistorting). In both urban and rural regions, the distributional shift is small but unambiguously regressive: as opposed to the nonneedy, the needy lose more from elimination of the subsidy (including leakage) than they gain from the tax cut.

Option 4: Target All Food Subsidies to Needy Households

Under this option, targeting is extended to all four subsidized food items, including *baladi* bread and wheat flour subsidies. Since Option 1 covers the discussion on targeting cooking oil and sugar subsidies, the targeting issues that are discussed here relate only to *baladi* bread and wheat flour subsidies (representing the remaining 77 percent of total food subsidy spending).

Targeting *baladi* bread and wheat flour subsidies to the needy (poor) would require a fundamental change in the operation of the *baladi* bread and wheat flour subsidy system. Under this reform, bakeries and warehouses would purchase 82 percent-extraction wheat flour from mills at an unsubsidized, free-market price. Bakeries would produce *baladi* bread from unsubsidized 82 percent-extraction wheat flour. Bakeries and warehouses would sell *baladi* bread and wheat flour to needy consumers at subsidized prices and to nonneedy (nonpoor) consumers at market prices. To implement this option, one major change that would need to be undertaken is that needy consumers would be required to bring with them to the bread outlets and warehouses proof or certification that they are eligible to receive *baladi* bread and wheat flour at subsidized prices. Such certification could take various forms: ration cards, coupons, tokens, food stamps, or plastic cards (with magnetized strips).

The government would distribute the certification cards, coupons, or tokens to poor families say every month through an administrative targeting scheme.[47] The amount of *baladi* bread or flour that could be purchased at subsidized prices would depend on family size. Each time they made a purchase, consumers would submit coupons or tokens to the bakeries and warehouses or subtractions would be made from ration books or magnetized cards, corresponding to the amount of *baladi* bread or flour purchased at subsidized prices. Bakeries and warehouses would redeem coupons, tokens, or other proof of sales for cash (the difference between the market price and the subsidized price) at banks or government offices.

Besides its expected impacts (reduced subsidy costs through better targeting and thus improved cost-effectiveness in transferring benefits to the needy), this targeting method would result in a major reform in the Egyptian wheat marketing sector. Supplying 82 percent-extraction wheat flour to bakeries and warehouses at an unsubsidized, free-market price would essentially de-link the food subsidy system from

---

[47] The administrative apparatus for certifying eligible households is a new, additional cost, for which a feasible, low-cost system, such as the proxy means tests developed by IFPRI for targeting rationed oil and sugar subsidy benefits, needs to be considered.

price interventions in the wholesale wheat flour market. Two IFPRI studies on wheat marketing and milling sectors indicate that de-linking the wheat marketing and milling sectors from the *baladi* bread and wheat flour subsidy system would remove a major barrier to wheat market liberalization. This would promote wheat milling and marketing efficiency and reduce government costs without jeopardizing consumer access to *baladi* bread and flour (Badiane, Kherallah, and Abdel-Latif 1998; Kherallah, Gruhn, and Abdel-Latif 1998).

Excluding the higher-income groups from all food subsidies is perceived to be politically unrealistic at present by senior government officials and a variety of social actors alike. Such a significant and far-reaching reform, although technically and administratively feasible, is not a major short-term priority of the Egyptian government. This option, however, may be pursued in the future.

Simulated Effects (Simulation 4). The results of Simulation 4 are summarized in Table 8.3. As expected, the effects are substantial (and much stronger than for Option 1, when only oil and sugar subsidies are targeted). Since bread and flour subsidies are not inframarginal (they influence the quantities consumed of bread and flour), an efficiency gain leads to a slight increase in aggregate consumption.

Food subsidy spending declines by 64 percent. The spending cut permits a significant reduction in income tax collection (by 16 percent). The redistribution of incomes in favor of the needy that follows from subsidy targeting generates increased demand for food and agricultural commodities, increased factor incomes in agriculture, and reduced incomes in nonagricultural sectors.[48,49] The final impact is a significant gain for the needy, especially in rural areas. However, it is not only the needy who see their position improve: the higher-income quintiles also gain. In every quintile, the rural population does better than its urban counterpart. The major losers are the urban third and fourth quintiles, who suffer from the subsidy cut and receive the bulk of their incomes from nonagricultural sources.

Higher prices for bread and flour reduce Egypt's wheat and flour imports (by 7 percent) but, because of substitution of other products and higher incomes for households with higher food budget shares, other food imports increase while food exports decrease. The ultimate decline in net food imports is less than 2 percent. The exchange rate appreciates slightly to maintain the *total* (food and nonfood) trade deficit fixed in foreign currency at the initial level. (See the discussion of macro system constraints in Appendix E.)

---

[48] Most of the simulations in this chapter involve changes from price subsidies (a negative indirect tax) to direct taxes (that is, shifts from a government tool that works through the price system to one that does not). Following Robinson and Thierfelder (1999), it is clear that such changes invariably generate declines in real factor returns that confuse the welfare analysis. For this reason, computed changes in the distribution of factor incomes are reported rather than absolute levels of factor incomes.

[49] See Appendix E, Table E.1 for the structure of household factor incomes according to the SAM for 1996/97 and for the base simulation.

Option 5: Eliminate All Food Subsidies

The complete elimination of the food subsidy is not currently a pressing issue from the perspective of government expenditures, because in recent years a gradual reform process has helped to reduce the level of subsidies as a percentage of expenditures. At the same time, the social safety-net function of food subsidies has increased during the ongoing economic reform and structural adjustment process. The political costs of eliminating all food subsidies may be too high. Policymakers are concerned that such a move would create social unrest. Therefore, this type of drastic reform is not a priority for the government.

Simulated Effects (Simulations 5a and 5b). As shown in Table 8.3, the elimination of all food subsidies (Simulation 5a) permits a cut in direct taxes by about 25 percent (reducing direct tax revenue by a value similar to the subsidy savings). The aggregate welfare gain is small but positive (a reflection that an efficiency gain follows from the cut in distorting bread and flour subsidies). The impact is strongly regressive: in both regions, the higher the household income quintile, the more positive the impact. As a result, consumption increases by 0.5 percent for nonneedy households and falls by 1.1 percent for the needy. The pattern of change is, however, strongly pro-rural—rural consumption increases by 0.6 percent while urban consumption declines slightly.

The main reason for the pro-rural pattern is that, as a result of the subsidy cut for bread and flour, households shift their demand from products based on wheat grain (a commodity without quality differences between imports and domestic production and, therefore, with perfect alignment between domestic and international prices) toward other food products (for which there are quality differences between domestic output sold at home and traded commodities). As a result, the prices of agricultural commodities for which demand increases are boosted, but the prices of agricultural commodities for which demand decreases do not decline. Higher agricultural prices and incomes disproportionately benefit rural households who, in turn, have higher budget shares for food. This causes a significant multiplier effect.

The shift in demand from wheat-based commodities that, on the margin, are imported toward other commodities necessitates an appreciation of the exchange rate (by 1.4 percent) to maintain the fixed current account and trade deficits. While wheat and flour imports decline significantly (by 7 percent), net food imports decline by much less.

The regressive distributional change for Simulation 5a suggests that full subsidy elimination is not an attractive option unless accompanied by measures that directly benefit the needy. In Simulation 5b, the savings from eliminating the subsidies are used to fund a transfer program targeted to the needy. According to the simulation, the transfer program receives more than LE 3.6 billion (that is, close to the value of the full subsidy program). The distributional impact inside each region is reversed as a result of the transfer. On the aggregate level, needy households gain 4.2 percent in real consumption, while the nonneedy incur a loss of 1.0 percent. The pro-rural pattern is reinforced, compared with Simulation 5a, because of the food-intensive demand pattern of the needy households who benefit from the transfer program. In foreign trade, the higher food import intensity in demand is reflected in roughly unchanged net food imports.

Option 6: Target **Baladi** *Bread Bakeries and Outlets to Poor Neighborhoods in Urban Areas*

The analysis in Chapter 5 suggested that the current concentration of *baladi* bread outlets relative to the number of people served is higher in richer neighborhoods than in poorer neighborhoods. *Baladi* bread subsidies can be better targeted to the poor if bakeries and distribution outlets are concentrated in poor neighborhoods. When the number of outlets is increased in poor urban neighborhoods, the number of *baladi* bread outlets in higher income neighborhoods may be reduced. This is a logistically feasible and low-cost form of targeting. However, this option may not be suitable for rural Egypt because there are no clear boundaries between "wealthier" and "poorer" neighborhoods in rural areas. Such boundaries are sometimes difficult to determine even in some urban areas.

The government may allow and encourage the bakeries in higher-income neighborhoods to produce and sell unsubsidized, improved-quality *baladi* bread made from 72 percent-extraction flour, along with subsidized *baladi* bread. This would mitigate the impact of the reduced supply of subsidized *baladi* bread in richer communities.

Option 7: Reallocate Subsidized Food Supply Among Governorates Using Poverty Levels as a Criterion

The analysis in Chapter 5 also showed that food subsidy allocations are not highly correlated with governorate-level poverty rates. Under this geographical targeting option, a two-step method could be followed. First, the total annual food subsidy resources could be better allocated to each governorate, according to its share of the country's total poverty. Allocation based only on total poverty rates is unlikely to be realistic, given the political factors that go into the equation, such as the urban bias. Second, at the governorate level, a larger proportion of the total subsidized foods received would be distributed to villages and urban areas where the poor are known to be concentrated. This would improve the accuracy of targeting.

A policy to increase the level of total subsidies to poorer regions can play a role in dampening political discontent by providing more social benefits to the poor, while not adding to bureaucratic procedures or creating new institutions. A difficulty with implementing this option is the likely opposition to such a plan from governorates who stand to lose a share of their subsidy benefits, assuming the total level of subsidy benefits remains unchanged.

Summary

This chapter provides a set of options for reforming Egypt's food subsidy system. These options have been analyzed from different angles, including simulation analysis with a CGE model of the Egyptian economy, to assess quantitatively the short-run economywide effects of alternative cost-saving scenarios for the food subsidy system.

The simulated impact of targeting or fully eliminating oil and sugar subsidies is relatively small, reflecting the limited size of this program. The savings permit a reduction in income taxes of 4–6 percent. The impact on disaggregated household welfare is also small (changes in real consumption for the different household types are between 0.2 percent and –0.3 percent). It is progressive if the subsidy is targeted to the needy and regressive if it is eliminated.

When similar measures are simulated for the entire food subsidy system, the impact is predictably much stronger, including important indirect effects. Nevertheless, although the current bread and flour subsidy program distorts consumer decisions, only minor efficiency gains follow from targeting or eliminating these subsidies.

In tandem with a direct tax cut, the targeting of all food subsidies has pro-needy and pro-rural effects. It raises the total consumption of the needy by 0.5 percent, with little change for the rest of the population. The strongest gains are recorded for the two lowest quintiles in rural areas, whose consumption goes up about 1.0 percent. Only the urban households in the third and fourth quintiles lose significantly, by 0.5–0.8 percent. This outcome is influenced by the redistribution of buying power in favor of needy households who allocate larger shares of their consumption to food. Increased demand for food items (other than wheat) raises agricultural prices and the incomes of the rural population in general and the poor in particular.

The distributional consequences of a full elimination of food subsidies in combination with a tax cut (reducing direct tax revenues by 25 percent) remain pro-rural; aggregate rural and urban consumption change by 0.6 percent for rural and –0.2 percent for urban dwellers. However, the pattern of welfare change is regressive. The nonneedy households enjoy a consumption increase of 0.5 percent, while the needy suffer a loss of 1.1 percent. But, if the savings from fully eliminating food subsidies are used instead for transfers to the needy, the household impact is drastically different. In addition to the transfer benefit, the rural needy gain strongly from demand shifts to and within agriculture, raising the consumption of the two lowest rural quintiles by 6–7 percent. On a more aggregate level, consumption increases by 1.2 percent for rural households and by 4.2 percent for needy households. Urban and nonneedy households register small losses.

The targeting or elimination of food subsidies has a significant impact on Egypt's foreign trade if the entire subsidy system is covered by the policy shifts. The declines are 6–7 percent for wheat and flour imports but much smaller for total net food and agricultural imports as a result of substitution effects on the consumption side.

Subsidy costs are reduced significantly when maize substitutes for 20 percent of the flour used to produce subsidized bread and flour, especially if leakage can be eliminated. Imports of wheat and flour and total net imports of food and agricultural items decline, especially if maize yields increase. If so, the gains in household well-being may also be noteworthy; if not, the impact is pro-rural but negligible.

Improved geographic targeting of food subsidies (Options 6 and 7) would bring greater benefits to the needy. Experience in some developing countries suggests that targeting by location is a logistically simple and low-cost method of targeting food subsidy and other social safety net programs.

In summary, the seven options discussed in this chapter are technically feasible and would save the government money to varying degrees depending on the option. These seven options fall into three groups in terms of their political feasibility. Targeting rationed oil and sugar subsidies to the needy (Option 1) and mixing maize and wheat flour at flour mills (Option 2) would most likely encounter little political opposition. Indeed, the policy of adding maize flour to wheat flour is already being implemented on an experimental basis. Options that suggest targeting *baladi* bread outlets to poor urban neighborhoods (Option 6), reallocating subsidies among governorates in accordance with poverty levels (Option 7), and eliminating the oil and sugar subsidies (Option 3) may incur significant opposition from some groups. Elimination of the oil and sugar subsidies would be particularly visible and likely to stimulate public debate. However, the magnitude of losses to those who would be hurt do not appear to be large. Therefore, these options may be politically feasible if, at some point, there is strong political will to carry them out.

Targeting all food subsidies to needy households (Option 4) and eliminating all food subsidies (Option 5) are not considered to be politically feasible options under present circumstances. The poor would be significantly hurt by the total elimination of food subsidies, so that within this third group, Option 4 may be more attractive to policymakers.

CHAPTER 9

Conclusions for Policy

IFPRI, in collaboration with the Egyptian Ministry of Agriculture and Land Reclamation (MALR) and Ministry of Trade and Supply (MOTS), conducted policy research on food security issues in Egypt over a three-year period starting in 1996. One of the primary objectives of this collaborative research was to evaluate the performance of the Egyptian food subsidy system and to identify policy options for reform of the system.

Since the mid-1980s, the Government of Egypt has used a variety of strategies to gradually reduce food subsidy costs. These strategies have included increasing the price of subsidized food commodities, reducing the number of ration card holders, and reducing both the number and quantity of subsidized food items available to consumers. As a result, the explicit cost of the food subsidy system has declined appreciably in real terms. Despite achieving a significant cost reduction, the absolute cost of food subsidies remains high, totaling LE 3.74 billion in 1996/97 in current prices, or about $1.1 billion.

How much of this $1.1 billion reaches the poor? To what extent is this a subsidy for the middle class? At the outset of the project, it was generally believed that subsidized *baladi* bread and *baladi* wheat flour were eaten more by low-income groups than by high-income groups and that the system was self-targeting, but no household-level data were available to confirm this widespread impression or to measure magnitudes. The food subsidy system had changed a great deal since it was last evaluated by IFPRI in the early 1980s. For example, subsidies had been removed from many food commodities, including *shami* bread, which is higher in quality than *baladi* bread. And the nominal price for *baladi* bread had increased from 1 to 5 piasters.

How much subsidized food, particularly *baladi* flour sold to bakers and sent to warehouse outlets for direct sale, was making its way into the private market without being sold at reduced prices—that is, how much leakage was there? Were government policies and controls effective in preventing leakage? Again, there were no data on which to base answers to these questions.

An obvious reform, in theory, is to move from a general, untargeted subsidy for *baladi* bread and wheat flour to a targeted system. The economic arguments for this type of reform are compelling, particularly if the present system was not self-targeting in terms of reaching the poor. But is it technically feasible? Could a means test be developed and reliably implemented? More important, could the political will be found to implement such a fundamental change—even if the poor were not harmed? Finding satisfying answers to these questions not only required formal interviews with policymakers and stakeholders, but also evolved over time through direct day-to-day contact with government officials as part of the collaborative project.

To address several of these key questions, the necessary first step was to undertake the Egypt Integrated Household Surveys described in Chapter 4. Based on data collected from these surveys and other sources, this report has reviewed the economic and political context of the food subsidy reform; analyzed key performance indicators of the food subsidy system, which together characterize the efficiency with which this system operates; and assessed several policy options, ranging from small, marginal, politically acceptable changes to the present system to a fundamental transformation to a fully targeted system.

How Well Does the Present System Target the Poor?

Broadly speaking, food subsidy benefits are about equally distributed across income groups. That is, 1 percent of the population receives more or less 1 percent of the subsidy benefits, irrespective of level of income. Given that the Egyptian food subsidy system is untargeted, evidence that the distribution of benefits are not skewed toward any particular income group is not surprising. Nevertheless, this pattern also suggests that the major proportion of subsidy benefits accrues to those who do not need it.[50] Consequently, the present general food subsidy system in Egypt represents an expensive means of trying to improve food security and nutrition of the poor.

Estimates in this study suggest that the value of total benefits from the food subsidy system going to the nonneedy was LE 1,933.5 million, or 51.7 percent of total food subsidy costs in 1996/97. As the combined result of system leakage and poor targeting, only about one-third of the total food subsidy incurred by the government goes to the needy, of which *baladi* bread accounts for 65 percent; wheat flour, 13 percent; sugar, 12 percent; and cooking oil, 10 percent.

Although there may be lower-cost ways of achieving the same objective, the current *baladi* bread subsidy nevertheless provides an effective means of transferring benefits to the poor, particularly the urban poor, helping to protect them against transitory shocks that may arise from the ongoing economic reform process in Egypt. Income benefits from food subsidies in urban areas amount to nearly 8 percent of total expenditures for the poorest 20 percent of households, 80 percent of which comes from purchase of subsidized *baladi* bread.

The current ration-card subsidy system for sugar and cooking oil is not well targeted. A majority of the more wealthy Egyptians (about 71 percent of households in

---

[50] The lowest two expenditure quintiles (bottom 40 percent of the population) are defined as needy, so the top three expenditure quintiles (top 60 percent of the population) are defined as nonneedy.

the top three expenditure quintiles) carry the more highly subsidized green ration cards, which are in principle intended for low-income households. These households receive about 62 percent of the total rationed subsidy benefits. On the other hand, about 10 percent of households in the poorest two quintiles hold the less subsidized red ration cards, which are intended for higher-income households. Indeed, about 14 percent of these poor households do not hold a ration card of any kind. The poor also receive less from rationed subsidy benefits than richer households, mainly because the government stopped registering newborns in 1989.

How Large a Problem Is Leakage?

Because of the high rates of price subsidy on the four items covered by the Egyptian food subsidy system, the incentive is quite strong to divert subsidized foods to the private market for sale at a higher price. Indeed, significant proportions of supplies of subsidized wheat flour (27.8 percent), sugar (19.6 percent), and cooking oil (15.4 percent) leaked before reaching the consumers. However, leakages from subsidized *baladi* bread at the national level were quite low—11.8 percent of the total supply.

How Cost-Effective Is the System in Reaching the Needy?

Overall, it costs the government LE 3.06 to transfer LE 1.00 of income to a needy household through its food subsidy system. The fiscal cost of each LE 1.00 transferred to general consumers through the *baladi* bread subsidy system is estimated to be LE 1.16—the lowest cost among the four subsidized foods. However, taking into consideration that 61 percent of the benefits from the *baladi* bread subsidy go to the nonneedy,[51] the cost increases to LE 2.98 to transfer LE 1.00 to a needy[52] household. In contrast, the rationed cooking oil subsidy system proved to be the least effective at directing income to consumers. The fiscal cost of transferring LE 1.00 of subsidy benefits to the needy through the cooking oil subsidy system is LE 4.64.

How Can Food Subsidies Be Better Targeted?

First, food subsidies can more effectively reach the poor if subsidized food distribution outlets are concentrated in poor neighborhoods. This analysis indicates that the concentration of *baladi* bread outlets relative to the number of people served is higher in richer neighborhoods than in poorer neighborhoods. This might be referred to as geographic targeting at the local level.

Second, this analysis reveals a strong urban bias in the allocation of food subsidies to various governorates. According to the 1996 census, 57 percent of the total

---

[51] If food subsidies are intended only for the needy, then the government bears the cost of leakage of these subsidies to the nonneedy population. Therefore, the cost of leakage of subsidies to the nonneedy is added to the cost of supplying subsidy benefits to the needy.

[52] Defining the lowest two quintiles, or bottom 40 percent, of the population as needy.

Egyptian population lived in rural areas, but only 30 percent of total food subsidies were allocated to rural areas in 1996/97. A major part of the difference in the allocation of benefits to urban and rural areas stems from the much larger quantities of *baladi* bread made available to urban dwellers. Moreover, governorate-level allocations are not sensitive to the geographic distribution of total poverty. Therefore, there is considerable scope for targeting food subsidies to the poor through geographic targeting at the governorate or regional level. Experience in other countries demonstrates that targeting by geographic area can be highly cost-effective and administratively simple.

Third, ration cards for subsidized sugar and oil can be made more progressive by providing green ration cards to low-income households who have no cards, by converting green cards of high-income households to red cards, by converting red cards of low-income households to green cards, and by reducing the subsidy paid to red card holders. In the event that the price subsidy were completely removed for red card holders, the red card would still function as an entitlement to a quantity ration in the event of a future emergency.

Fourth, mixing maize flour with *baladi* wheat flour at the milling site would prevent leakage of subsidized flour before it reaches consumers, because the mixed flour cannot be sifted down to higher-quality 72 percent-extraction wheat flour for eventual sale on the open market. This has already been implemented in selected bakeries on an experimental basis starting in late 1996. Recently, this experimentation has been extended to subsidized flour sold to consumers through warehouses. The government's main objective in this initiative is to decrease the wheat import bill and the cost of subsidizing wheat consumption (maize flour is less expensive than wheat flour).

Who Is "Poor" and Who Is "Nonpoor"?

In any administrative targeting effort, the major challenge facing policymakers is to develop an accurate system for identifying the poor and the nonpoor members of the society. What criteria should the managers of the food subsidy system use to identify the poor and the nonpoor? Do the benefits of targeting food subsidies justify the cost of collecting information that is needed for targeting?

The per capita income of a household can be considered a measure of the household's welfare. However, verifying income levels is difficult to do in Egypt and in other developing countries because reliable records needed for verification usually do not exist. Measurement of household income or expenditure requires expensive and time-consuming surveys, therefore, rigorous tests of household welfare or "means" to determine eligibility and benefit levels for a program are rarely used in developing countries.

An alternative method of measuring household welfare is to carry out a "proxy means test." This approach relies on indicators that are highly correlated with household income, yet are easy to collect, observe, and verify. Points can be assigned to the selected indicators and eligibility assigned on the basis of the score, as a proxy for means or income. A comparative study of 30 targeted social programs in Latin

America reveals that, among all targeting mechanisms, the proxy means test used in Chile resulted in the highest targeting rate to the poor.

At the request of MOTS, the IFPRI research team of the Food Security Research Project in Egypt developed a proxy means test for targeting rationed food subsidies. Using data collected through the 1997 EIHS as part of the project, a regression model was developed that identified nine variables strongly associated with household income. These indicators were subsequently field tested and a proxy means test finalized. An ex ante evaluation of the levels of accuracy of the proxy means test indicated that 72 percent of those who were actually needy were correctly predicted as needy, giving a 28 percent error of exclusion of the needy. Only 16 percent of the actual nonneedy were inaccurately designated as needy. With a zero exclusion error, the proxy means test identifies 58 percent of the population as needy (Ahmed et al. 1999).

Under this method, it would be possible to use the estimated coefficients of the indicators from the regression equation to predict household eligibility for subsidized sugar and cooking oil distributed through the ration card system. Officials from the MOTS food subsidy system could collect data on the indicators from households, which would be substituted into formulas derived from the estimated regression equation, and eligibility could be determined.

What Are Politically Feasible Policy Options for Reform?

Given the absence of any pressing need for far-reaching change in the food subsidy system, more politically sensitive policy options—such as increasing the price of *baladi* bread to eliminate subsidy or developing a targeted bread subsidy system using food stamps or coupons—are perceived to be unrealistic at this time both by senior government officials and a variety of stakeholders. At present, there are a number of politically feasible options that would also result in improved targeting and cost savings. These may be divided into two groups, based on the degree of political opposition that they might encounter.

The first group of options would likely encounter little political opposition. These include "cleaning" the ration card system by increasing benefits to the poor and reducing benefits to the rich, and mixing maize flour with *baladi* wheat flour to reduce leakage.

The second group of options is perceived to be more politically sensitive. These options include eliminating the sugar and oil subsidies, targeting outlets in poor neighborhoods, and redirecting governorate-level allocations so that they are more closely aligned with the levels of poverty found in those governorates. Because elimination of the oil and sugar subsidies would be particularly visible, it would be conducive to public debate. However, the magnitude of losses to those who would be hurt do not appear to be large, so these options may be politically feasible if at some point there is strong political will to carry them out.

APPENDIX A

Method for Estimating Food Subsidy Cost

In this report, the fiscal or budgetary costs of the food subsidy system are calculated. The cost is defined as the gross cost minus revenue, which is equal to the total subsidy, or net cost, of the system. While gross cost has to be based on figures on the supply side (that is, domestic procurement, import, change in stock, and loss), the revenue estimates flow from the demand side (that is, the sales from the system).

The prices used for estimating the budgetary cost are the c.i.f. (cost, insurance, freight) import price for imported quantity, the procurement price for domestically procured quantity, the selling price of bran (a by-product of the 82 percent-extraction wheat flour), and the subsidized selling prices of commodities to bakeries, warehouses, and ration (*tamween*) shops. The official exchange rate is used in the conversion of the foreign import price to domestic currency (LE).

The gross cost consists of (1) food purchase costs (both domestic and imported); (2) internal transport, storage, and handling costs; (3) administrative costs (salaries and services); (4) actual interest payments on capital; and (5) transfer payments (that is, custom duties for imports and taxes). Transfer payments are included in the budgetary cost calculation but excluded from the economic cost calculation.

The change in stock, which represents opening stock minus closing stock in any given year, is not taken into account in the subsidy cost calculation in this report. A comparison between total procurement (import and domestic) and total distribution in any given year shows very little difference. Since opening and closing stocks may include both imported and domestically procured quantities, and imports and domestic procurements are made at different time periods in a year while distributions occur throughout the year, it is difficult, if not impossible, to accurately value change in stock.

For purposes of illustration, the actual subsidy cost calculations for the 82 percent-extraction wheat flour for production of subsidized *baladi* bread in 1996/97 are presented in Table A.1.

Table A.1—Calculation of the subsidy cost for the 82 percent-extraction wheat flour supplied to bakeries for subsidized *baladi* bread production, 1996/97

Item	Quantity	Price or unit value	Cost and revenue
	(1,000 metric tons)	(LE/metric ton)	(million LE)
Gross cost calculation			
Imported wheat, and c.i.f. price	3,488.14	657.74	2,294.29
Custom duties and taxes on imported wheat	3,488.14	22.31	77.82
Domestically procured wheat, and procurement price	881.19	667.00	587.75
Internal transport and handling costs	4,369.33	16.77	73.27
Storage cost	4,369.33	27.15	118.63
Milling cost	4,369.33	47.93	209.42
Administrative and service costs	4,369.33	33.86	147.94
Interest cost	4,369.33	20.44	89.31
Gross cost	...	...	3,598.43
Revenue calculation			
Total clean wheat for milling (net of transport and handling losses, dust, and other foreign materials)	4,165.90	...	...
Bran (a by-product of 82 percent-extraction flour) and bran price	749.86	400.00	299.94
Wheat flour (82 percent extraction) and subsidized selling price to bakeries	3,416.04	290.00	990.65
Total revenue	...	...	1,290.60
Subsidy cost (gross cost minus revenue)	...	...	2,307.83

Source: Calculated from data provided by the Ministry of Trade and Supply.
Note: Ellipsis (. . .) indicates not applicable.

APPENDIX B

Estimating the Profitability of *Baladi* Bread Production

Bakeries, mostly private, play one of the most important institutional roles in the *baladi* bread subsidy system.[53] *Baladi* wheat flour is sold to bakeries at subsidized prices. As described previously, bakeries are then expected to produce a specified number of loaves per sack of flour purchased, at a specified weight, and to sell loaves at a specified price. The opportunity presents itself for circumventing these regulations and diverting subsidized wheat flour to the private market, which is a form of "leakage." Is there a strong incentive to divert flour to the private market? How profitable are bakeries if they follow the stipulated rules?

The community survey described in Chapter 4 obtained detailed information on the costs of subsidized *baladi* bread production. The community survey collected information from 125 urban and rural bakeries and outlets in 20 governorates. In Table B.1, the costs are broken down by region. The cost of wheat flour is the largest item, accounting for 61.8 percent of total bread production cost on average. Labor constitutes the next most important cost item (15.9 percent). Labor cost is relatively high in the metropolitan region. Transport cost per sack of flour is highest in the upper rural region because of the relatively longer distance from the source of wheat flour supply.[54] On average, the cost of production per loaf of *baladi* bread is estimated at 4.70 piasters, ranging from 4.54 piasters in the lower urban areas to 4.84 piasters in the metropolitan areas. The bakeries sell *baladi* bread to consumers at the price of 5 piasters per loaf.

---

[53] See Chapter 3 for a description of how bakeries operate.

[54] The average distance of a bakery from its source of wheat flour supply (both government-run and private flour mills) is 10.8 kilometers, but it varies widely across regions. The average distance is 6.2 kilometers in the metropolitan region, 9.2 kilometers in the lower urban region, 16.6 kilometers in the lower rural region, 4.6 kilometers in the upper urban region, and 11.4 kilometers in the upper rural region. Loss of wheat flour during transportation and handling averaged 2.5 kilograms per a 100-kilogram sack of flour.

Table B.1—Costs of subsidized *baladi* bread production, by bakeries

Cost item	Metropolitan	Lower urban	Lower rural	Upper urban	Upper rural	Average	Share of cost
	(LE/100 kilograms of flour or 1,000 loaves of bread)						(percent)
Wheat flour	29.00	29.00	29.00	29.00	29.00	29.00	61.8
Transportation	0.90	0.94	1.11	1.06	1.22	1.05	2.2
Labor	8.95	6.40	7.12	7.50	7.39	7.47	15.9
Ingredients	3.76	2.86	2.89	2.89	2.98	3.08	6.6
Bran	2.49	1.46	1.35	1.56	1.56	1.68	3.6
Yeast	0.95	0.99	1.29	0.95	1.04	1.04	2.2
Salt	0.32	0.41	0.28	0.38	0.34	0.35	0.8
Fuel and power	3.66	4.32	5.49	3.92	2.23	3.92	8.4
Maintenance	0.47	0.28	0.41	0.48	0.61	0.45	1.0
Rent	0.55	0.72	1.07	1.22	0.95	0.90	1.9
Outlet commission	1.10	0.92	1.22	1.10	1.14	1.10	2.3
Total	48.39	45.44	48.31	47.17	45.52	46.97	100.0
Cost/loaf (piasters)	4.84	4.54	4.83	4.72	4.55	4.70	

Source: IFPRI Food Security Research Project in Egypt, the Community Survey component of the "Egypt Integrated Household Survey, 1997."

Table B.2 provides average monthly profitability of *baladi* bread production for the bakeries by region. Profit or net income per month represents what is left after expenses incurred in production of *baladi* bread have been deducted from the revenues earned on the sale of bread.[55] The average profit per bakery was LE 756 per month. Monthly profit was lowest for the bakeries in the lower rural areas (LE 241 per bakery) and highest in the lower urban areas (LE 1,178 per bakery). The regional variation in profit results from the regional variations in the average quota of wheat flour per bakery and the average bread production cost. In 1997, the average quota of wheat flour per bakery ranged from 14.3 metric tons per month in the lower rural areas to 38.6 metric tons per month in the metropolitan areas (Table B.2).

The return on investment is determined by dividing the profit by the operating expenses, after interest on operating expenses has been subtracted from profit.[56] The

[55] The profitability calculation does not include the extra profit obtained by circumventing the regulations, that is, through unauthorized sales of subsidized *baladi* wheat flour by bakeries at a higher than subsidized price. Chapter 6 of this report shows that this system leakage was about 12 percent of the total quantity of *baladi* wheat flour supplied to bakeries in 1997.

[56] The bank lending rate for commercial activities was 14 percent per year in 1997. The bakeries were assumed to receive short-term credit at an annual interest rate of 14 percent. The bakers were to repay the loan at the end of every month, so they needed to pay interest for only that period, that is, the amount of interest per month was only one-twelfth of 14 percent. The average interest on operating expenses is calculated as follows: first, divide the interest rate in decimal terms by 12, then multiply the amount of monthly operating expenses by that number [$12{,}098 \times (0.14/12)$] = 141.14. So, the profit after interest is (756 – 141.14) = 614.86 per month. The return on investment is [$(614.86/12{,}098) \times 100$] = 5.1 percent per month or 61.2 percent per year.

Table B.2—Average profitability to bakeries of *baladi* bread production, by region, 1997

Item	Metropolitan	Lower urban	Lower rural	Upper urban	Upper rural	Average
Total number of bakeries	2,567	2,704	1,544	2,049	1,431	. . .
Total supply of flour to bakeries (tons/month)	99,191.7	69,860.0	22,021.7	61,058.3	28,616.7	. . .
Quantity of flour per bakery (tons/month)	38.6	25.8	14.3	29.8	20.0	25.7
Bread production cost (LE/bakery/month)	18,698.4	11,740	6,890	14,056.2	9,103	12,098
Revenue (LE/bakery/month)	19,321	12,918	7,131	14,900	9,999	12,854
Profit (LE/bakery/month)	622	1,178	241	843	895	756

Sources: Calculated by the authors from Table B.1; the number of bakeries and subsidized flour supply data are from the Ministry of Trade and Supply.

Note: Ellipsis (. . .) indicates not applicable.

average return on investment is 5.1 percent per month, or 61.2 percent per year, which is a conservative estimate of the return on investment.[57] Although most bakers complain about rising wages and costs of other inputs, this analysis suggests that bakeries are profitable enterprises even without the diversion of subsidized flour to the black market for earning extra profit. This is consistent with the increasing demand for bakery ownership throughout Egypt.

On average, the bakeries operate 7.2 hours per day. The hours of operation by region are metropolitan, 9.9 hours; lower urban, 8.3 hours; lower rural, 5.1 hours; upper urban, 11.7 hours; and upper rural, 5.5 hours. Bakeries produce an average of 1,025 loaves of *baladi* bread from a sack of 100 kilograms of wheat flour. Bakers reported that, on average, about 1 percent of the total amount of bread produced remained unsold because of defects (for example, burnt, not well-baked, and so forth). On average, each bakery employs 10.2 workers. Regional patterns of employment per bakery are metropolitan, 12.8 workers; lower urban, 12.5 workers; lower rural, 6.7 workers; upper urban, 14.6 workers; and upper rural, 8.3 workers. Regional variation in employment per bakery arises mainly due to the regional variation in the average quota of wheat flour per bakery.

Most of the bakeries (75.2 percent) have semi-electric ovens, followed by manual ovens (21.6 percent). Only 3.2 percent of the bakeries have fully electric ovens. The community survey results suggest that 65.6 percent of the total number of bakeries are owned, while the remainder (34.4 percent) are rented. Virtually all bakers

[57] It is assumed that the turnover of operating capital requires one month. However, bakers reported that they had lifted their quota of subsidized wheat flour 23 times per month, on average, so that the rate of turnover of operating capital should be much quicker than what is assumed. Even this conservative estimate of annual return on investment for the bakeries is quite high (61.2 percent) compared with the interest rate on borrowed capital (14 percent).

(99.2 percent) reported that they baked only subsidized *baladi* bread in their bakeries. Most of the *baladi* bread sales outlets (69.8 percent) are located either inside the bakeries or are attached to the bakeries.

Outlets sell an average of 10,113 loaves of *baladi* bread per day. Daily sales of loaves per outlet vary widely across the regions: metropolitan, 17,976 loaves; lower urban, 13,732 loaves; lower rural, 8,504 loaves; upper urban, 11,110 loaves; and upper rural, 6,561 loaves. Only 0.32 percent of the total number of loaves received by outlets from bakeries remained unsold. About 48 percent of the unsold bread was sold the next day at a lower price as animal feed, and the remainder was either consumed by outlet employees or given away.

Under the rules and regulations set out by the government, then, baking and selling subsidized *baladi* bread appears to be a highly profitable operation. If individual bakers were to divert large quantities of *baladi* wheat flour to the private market, they would risk losing their daily quotas and right to operate, thus risking loss of the profits they now receive and perhaps a jail term. The low levels of leakage estimated in this report are consistent with the incentives not to circumvent government rules and regulations.

APPENDIX C

Leakage Estimation Method and Data

The magnitude of leakages in the Egyptian food subsidy system can be approximated by subtracting the total quantities of subsidized *baladi* bread (wheat flour equivalent), wheat flour, sugar, and cooking oil that were actually purchased by consumers during the household survey in March–May 1997 (IFPRI's EIHS data) from the quantities of these commodities that MOTS put into the system during the same period. The difference between supply and purchases measures the extent of leakage in the system. This method of estimating leakages as a residual has been used in studies on general food subsidy systems in other countries (see Ahluwalia 1993; Rajagopalan 1989; Alderman, Chaudhry, and Garcia 1988).

Average per capita purchases of subsidized *baladi* bread, wheat flour, sugar, and cooking oil at subsidized prices were estimated from the data generated by the nationally representative EIHS conducted by IFPRI in collaboration with MALR and MOTS in March–May 1997. The survey consisted of a sample of 2,500 households drawn from 125 urban and rural primary sampling units (PSUs) in 20 governorates. Each PSU represents either an urban *shiakha* or a rural village. The sample frame used for the selection of households was supplied by CAPMAS. A description of the EIHS is provided in Chapter 4 of this report.

Since the EIHS data were representative of the PSUs, it was possible to estimate the PSU-level total purchases of each of the subsidized foods by multiplying the average per capita purchases in a PSU with the population of that PSU, which could then be summed to provide aggregate regional-level or national-level estimates of subsidized food consumption. Total population in a PSU has been estimated as follows. The 1995 listing of households from the CAPMAS master sample frame gives the total number of households in each PSU (*shiakha*/village). Based on this listing, the total number of households in each PSU for 1997 was estimated using a 2.2 percent population growth rate. Next, the 1997 population in each PSU was calculated by multiplying the 1997 estimates of the total number of households in each PSU with the average household size in that PSU obtained from the 1997 EIHS data.

IFPRI conducted a community survey in June 1997 in the same 125 PSUs where the household survey was conducted. In this survey, data on total quantities of subsidized wheat flour supplied to bakeries and warehouses and subsidized sugar and cooking oil supplied to ration (*tamween*) shops during March–May 1997 in each of the 125 *shiakhas* and villages were obtained from the local offices of MOTS.

Bakers are required to produce 10 loaves of *baladi* bread from one kilogram of wheat flour, each loaf weighing 130 grams. In the community survey, weights of loaves purchased from subsidized *baladi* bread outlets were measured using weighing scales. Flour-equivalent *baladi* bread purchases were estimated using information on the official specification and measured weights of *baladi* bread. If the actual weight of a loaf was lower than 130 grams, then the difference was converted to flour equivalence, and added to leakage estimates.

APPENDIX D

Mathematical Formulation for the Food Demand Model, Based on Demand for Characteristics

Utility is a function of the energy, variety, and taste (characteristics of the food consumed) and of nonfood purchases. Total utility gained from these three characteristics and from nonfoods is the weighted sum of the individual utilities that these four items generate.

$$U = w_e U_e(E) + w_v U_v(V) + \sum_{i=1}^{n} w_{ti} U_{ti}(q_i) + w_{nf} U_{nf}(q_{nf}), \tag{1}$$

where

U	=	total utility from all food and nonfood goods,
q	=	quantity of a good,
i	=	1, . . ., n are the n foods consumed,
E	=	a measure of energy in the diet,
V	=	a measure of variety in the diet,
U_e	=	utility derived from energy,
U_v	=	utility derived from variety,
$U_{ti}(q_i)$	=	utility derived from the taste of q units of good i,
$U_{nf}(q_{nf})$	=	utility derived from q units of the nonfood good,
w_e	=	weight placed on utility from energy,
w_v	=	weight placed on utility from variety,
w_{ti}	=	weight placed on taste from individual food i,
w_{nf}	=	weight placed on utility from the nonfood good.

Utility from Energy (E)

$$E = \sum_{i=1}^{n} z_i q_i, \qquad (2)$$

where

z_i = factor converting quantity of the ith food into calories. E is total calories consumed per adult equivalent.

$$U_e(E) = e_2 E + e_3 E^2, \qquad (3)$$

where $e_2 > 0$ and $e_3 < 0$.

At low levels of total energy, each additional unit of energy increases utility, but at a decreasing rate. The functional form chosen, however, allows for marginal decreases in utility from additional units of energy at sufficiently high intakes of energy.

$$E_i = w_e(e_2 z_i + 2e_3 E z_i) > 0 \text{ for low-income groups} \qquad (4)$$

where

$$E_i = \frac{\partial U}{\partial U_e(E)} \frac{\partial U_e(E)}{\partial q_i}.$$

$$E_{ij} = 2 w_e e_3 z_i z_j < 0, \qquad (5)$$

where

$$E_{ij} = \frac{\partial E_i}{\partial q_j}.$$

Analogous notation will be used below for V_i, V_{ij}, T_i, and T_{ij}.

Utility from Taste (T)

$$U_{ti}(q_i) = \log(q_i), \qquad (6)$$

$$T_i = w_{ti}\left(\frac{1}{q_i}\right) > 0, \qquad (7)$$

$$T_{ii} = - w_{ti}\left(\frac{1}{q_i}\right)^2 < 0, \qquad (8)$$

$$T_{ij} = 0. \tag{9}$$

Each additional unit of taste of good *i,* no matter what the quantity, adds additional utility, but at a decreasing rate. The first derivative is positive and the second derivative negative, which is similar to energy for low-income groups. For taste, however, the "across food" second derivative is zero.

Utility from Variety (V)

$$U_v(V) = \frac{M}{R}, \tag{10}$$

where
M = nonstaple kilograms of food consumed per adult equivalent, and
R = total kilograms of food consumed per adult equivalent.

$$V_i = \frac{-w_v M}{R^2} < 0 \quad \text{for } i \leq s, \tag{11}$$

$$V_i = w_v\left(\frac{1}{R}\right)\left(1 - \left[\frac{M}{R}\right]\right) > 0 \quad \text{for } s < i < n,$$

where $i = 1, \ldots, s$ are staple foods.

Each additional unit of a staple good reduces utility from variety and each additional unit of a nonstaple good increases utility from variety.

$$V_{ij} = \frac{2M}{R^3} > 0 \quad \text{for } i, j \leq s; \tag{12}$$

$$V_{ij} = \left(\frac{w_v}{R^3}\right)[2M - R] \quad \text{for } i \leq s \text{ and } s < j < n;$$

$$V_{ij} = \left(\frac{2w_v}{R^3}\right)[M - R] < 0 \quad \text{for } s \leq i, j < n.$$

For all three sets of *i* and *j*, $V_{ij} = V_{ji}$.

Solving the Model

For any food *i:*

$$p_i = \frac{\partial U/\partial U_e}{\lambda}\left[\frac{\partial U_e}{\partial E}\frac{\partial E}{\partial q_i}\right] + \frac{\partial U/\partial U_v}{\lambda}\left[\frac{\partial U_v}{\partial V}\frac{\partial V}{\partial q_i}\right] + \frac{\partial U/\partial U_T}{\lambda}\left[\frac{\partial U_T}{\partial T}\frac{\partial T}{\partial q_i}\right] i = 1, \ldots, n, \tag{13}$$

where

P_i = price of food i,

λ = Lagrangian multiplier derived from the budget constraint.

There are n equations associated with (13), which for the first food, a staple, gives

$$p_1 = \frac{w_b}{\lambda}\left[e_2 z_1 + 2e_3 z_1 E\right] + \frac{w_v}{\lambda}\left[\frac{-M}{R^2}\right] + \frac{w_{t1}}{\lambda}\left[\frac{1}{q_1}\right]. \quad (14)$$

Shadow prices for energy and variety are given by the product of the coefficient outside the brackets times the first derivative inside the brackets, for the first and second terms in equation (14), respectively. Generally, shadow prices will decrease with increased consumption as the first derivative declines. However, the marginal utility of income, λ, declines with income, tending to raise the shadow price.

Elasticity estimates do not depend on λ but on the flexibility of the marginal utility of income, ϕ, a term that involves λ and that is used in the Frisch technique for estimating demand elasticities (Pinstrup-Andersen, de Londono, and Hoover 1976). Thus, there are $(n + 5)$ unknowns associated with the n equations represented by equation (13), specifically w_e, w_v, e_2, e_3, and the n w_{ti}s. An additional equation for the nonfood good (which includes ϕ as an unknown) gives a total of $(n + 1)$ equations. Prior specification of four elasticities identifies the four "extra" parameters.

APPENDIX E

The Computable General Equilibrium Model

Model Structure

Disaggregation

In Chapter 8, Table 8.1 shows the disaggregation of institutions, factors, and activities in the model. Among the factors, labor and capital are used by all sectors, while water, summer land, and winter land are used only by agricultural crop activities. The crop activities are differentiated according to period of land occupation into winter crops, summer crops, and perennial crops. Outside agriculture, there is a one-to-one mapping between activities (the producing sectors) and commodities (the outputs produced). Inside agriculture, the two berseem activities and the two vegetable activities are both assumed to produce the same commodity (berseem and vegetables, respectively). Given the quality difference between domestic maize (about 95 percent white maize) and imported (yellow) maize, the latter is a separate commodity that is not produced domestically; it is only imported. Moreover, several crop activities create by-products that are used as animal feed. This disaggregation of agriculture makes it possible to capture direct links between crop and animal activities: crop outputs (most importantly berseem, maize, and various crop by-products) are used as inputs in the animal activity; animal outputs (manure and animal labor) are used as inputs in crop activities.

Production, Factors, and Factor Markets

In crop agriculture, it is assumed that, apart from agronomic and institutional restrictions (which are described later), the factors land (summer and winter), water, and capital (primarily agricultural machinery) are mobile across crops and allocated so as to equalize the marginal returns to each factor in all relevant crops. In animal agriculture, capital use (primarily animals) is fixed and specific to this sector. For two factor types, land and water, excess supply is possible; if so, the price is zero. The other factors—agricultural labor, crop capital, and animal capital—are fully utilized with flexible market-clearing wages and rents.[58]

Outside of agriculture, capital quantities are fixed by activity; flexible rents ensure that these quantities are fully employed. Nonagricultural labor, the market of which is separate from the agricultural labor market, is mobile across nonagricultural sectors. Labor employment is fixed at the level observed in 1996/97, while a flexible wage also clears this part of the labor market.

For selected factors (summer and winter land and nonagricultural labor), the prices (the rents or the wages) are differentiated across the demanding activities on the basis of fixed ratios (calculated from base-year data). This is a reflection of real-world phenomena that are not modeled explicitly.[59] When the (aggregate) factor price changes, this is accompanied by proportional changes in the differentiated activity-specific prices of the factor in question.

The production technologies are summarized in Figure E.1. Producers are assumed to maximize profits, given the prices of inputs and outputs and their technology, which is specified by a nested Constant Elasticity of Substitution (CES) value-added function and Leontief intermediate input coefficients that are flexible inside agriculture but fixed for other sectors. The arguments of the value-added functions are labor, capital, and (for the crop sectors) a land/water aggregate. The latter is made up of land and water in fixed proportions. Thus, for crops, substitutability is possible between labor, capital, and the land/water aggregate on the level of the value-added functions; there is no substitutability between land and water.

The model accounts for two major agronomic area constraints: the area of short berseem (a crop that precedes cotton) is constrained to equal the cotton area, and the cotton area is limited to a maximum of one-third of the land not covered by perennial crops. Given the relatively short-run time frame of the analysis, the areas of perennial crops and, as noted above, the size of animal stock are fixed. Agricultural intermediate input coefficients are flexible in the context of producer minimization of intermediate input costs subject to a limited degree of input substitutability (given by a CES function) and a fixed *aggregate* input requirement per unit of the activity. Agriculture deviates from the more standard treatment for other sectors to avoid rigid links between crop and animal activities in Egypt's agriculture, as crop activities supply the animal activity with the bulk of its intermediate feed inputs.[60]

---

[58] Given that the quantity of water stored in the High Dam at Aswan is high, the water supply is set at a level that is above the quantity demanded for any of the simulations presented in this chapter. Hence, land is always in scarce supply. For water, the model records consumption by crop at a scarcity value of zero.

[59] For labor, wage gaps between activities may be linked to differences in job security, educational requirements, status of job, and physical (dis)comfort. In agriculture, recorded monetary returns to land may differ as crops differ in required skills, monitoring, riskiness, and impact on soil fertility.

[60] Given that fodder by-products from crop activities are not traded internationally, fixed intermediate input coefficients would, for the animal activity, generate rigid links between, on the one hand, the level of animal production and, on the other hand, the levels for the crop activities producing these by-products. Similar rigidities would appear if intermediate crop demands for manure were a fixed coefficient.

Figure E.1—Production technology

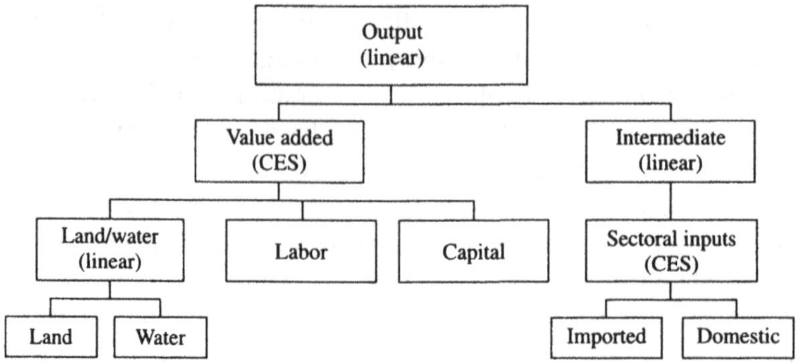

Two nonagricultural sectors are given special treatment. For the oil activity, the quantities of output and factor use are fixed at the 1997 level (treating these decisions as exogenous to the model). For electricity, a flexible capital supply (reflecting surplus capacity) ensures that the nontraded electricity commodity is sold at a fixed price.

Domestic Institutions: Households and Government

The model captures the circular flow of incomes in the economy. The income of each factor, generated by the production activities or transferred from the rest of the world (fixed in foreign currency), is split among the domestic institutions in fixed factor-specific shares.[61] In addition to factor incomes, households receive transfers from the government and the rest of the world (fixed in foreign currency). Household income is used to pay direct taxes, save, and consume. Direct taxes and savings are fixed and flexible shares of household income, respectively. (The reason for the flexible savings share will be discussed further on.) Disaggregated consumption is determined by a nested demand system. On the top level, the Almost Ideal Demand System (AIDS) generates demand for disaggregated food items and an aggregated nonfood item. At the lower level, Linear Expenditures System (LES) demand functions split aggregated nonfood demand into disaggregated items.[62]

Besides factor incomes, government revenue consists of transfers from the rest of the world (fixed in foreign currency) and taxes—direct taxes from households, indirect taxes from domestic activities, sales tax revenues, and import tariffs. All taxes are ad valorem. On the government spending side, transfers to households and the value of aggregate government consumption are fixed shares of nominal GDP. On the disaggregated level, the government consumes commodities in fixed proportions; the

[61] Low-income households rely more heavily on labor income, in rural areas, from work in agriculture; high-income households receive the bulk of their incomes from capital and, in rural areas, land.

[62] For a discussion of these functional forms, see Deaton and Muellbauer 1980.

consumed quantities for each commodity are scaled by a common factor to ensure that the required aggregate consumption value is reached. In addition, the government subsidizes part of household consumption of foodstuffs, transportation, and electricity. For the two nonfoods, the subsidy is a fixed share of the price paid by the consumer.

The treatment of food subsidies is of particular importance. The subsidized food items are disaggregated into subsidized bread, subsidized flour (purchased by consumers and used as an input in the production of subsidized bread), and other processed food (representing oil and sugar). Subsidized bread and flour are available to consumers at fixed prices in nonrationed quantities. Flexible subsidy rates also ensure that the consumer price remains unchanged when market conditions change. Given that subsidized oil and sugar are rationed and, for most households, supplemented by market purchases, the subsidy on other processed food has little direct impact on the quantities consumed of these commodities. Hence, it is treated as a cash transfer from the government to the households, with the value received by each household corresponding to the benefit it received from the oil and sugar subsidy in 1996/97. As a result of leakages, part of the subsidy does not reach the households through the intended channels. In the model, the part of the subsidy benefit that is leaked is distributed to households in the same way as nonagricultural capital incomes. This is compatible with the assumption that, at some point in the marketing channel, the subsidized items are sold at full market prices, generating profits for retailers and traders, that is, owners of capital in the nonagricultural part of the economy (a relatively high-income part of the population).

The Rest of the World, Foreign Trade, and Commodity Markets

In addition to transferring money that adds to or deducts from the incomes of domestic institutions, the rest of the world supplies imports and demands exports. For vegetables and services, exports are demanded according to constant-elasticity demand curves—the lower the export supply price, the larger the quantity exported. For all other commodities, Egypt is able to export or import any quantity it desires at international prices that are fixed in foreign currency.

For imports of wheat and exports of rice and oil, it is assumed that domestic output sold domestically and traded (exported or imported) commodities are perfect substitutes. As a result, as long as these commodities are traded (which they are for the simulations in this chapter), the domestic price is determined by the domestic-currency export or import price (transformed from the foreign currency price via the exchange rate and adjusted for any trade taxes or subsidies). The quantities exported or imported are market-clearing residuals.

Apart from the above-mentioned special treatment for wheat, rice, and oil, imperfect substitutability or transformability is assumed for foreign trade. The Armington assumption is used to capture the choice between imports and domestic output under imperfect substitutability: If a commodity is imported, all domestic demands—household and government consumption, investment demand, and intermediate demand—are for the same composite commodity. The mix between imports and domestic output determined by the assumption that domestic demanders minimize cost subject to import and domestic output prices in a setting with imperfect substitutability between commodities from these two sources, is captured by a CES aggregation function. Similarly, the allocation of domestic output between exports and domestic sales is determined on the assumption that domestic producers maximize profits subject to export and domestic sales prices in a setting with imperfect transformability between these two market outlets. This allocation is expressed by a constant-elasticity-of-transformation (CET) function. These assumptions—imperfect substitutability and transformability—grant the domestic price system a certain degree of independence from international prices and dampen export and import responses to changes in the producer environment. For these commodities, the markets for domestic outputs sold domestically are cleared by flexible domestic prices, influencing the quantities demanded (domestic demand from the Armington function) and the quantities supplied (domestic supply from the CET function). Finally, as noted, for the nontraded electricity commodity, the quantity supplied clears the market, given that supply is infinitely elastic at the fixed base price.

Macro System Constraints

The macro system constraints (or macro closures) determine the manner in which the accounts for the government, the rest of the world, and savings investment are brought into balance.[63]

Government savings (also called the current government surplus) are invariably fixed.[64] For most simulations, a change in the direct tax rate (the change in the rate is uniform across all households) ensures that government savings are maintained at the predetermined level. In the balance of the rest of the world, foreign savings (the current account deficit) are similarly fixed; the exchange rate (the price of foreign exchange) is the equilibrating variable. Given that all nontrade items (transfers to or from domestic institutions or factors) are fixed, fixing foreign savings is equivalent to fixing the trade deficit. On the spending side of the savings-investment balance, aggregate investment is fixed in quantity terms. On the savings side, uniform changes in the savings rates of each household category are used to generate a level of total savings needed to finance aggregate investment.[65]

---

[63] The rules for clearing the micro system constraints (the micro closures) were described in the discussion of factor and commodity markets.

[64] Government savings are invariably positive, given that they refer to the difference between *current* revenues and *current* spending, excluding items on the government *capital* account.

[65] Savings from nonhousehold sources—the government and the rest of the world—are not free to equilibrate aggregate savings investment. Given that real investment (foreign currency), foreign savings, and government savings are all fixed, the changes in household savings rates are very small.

The model is homogeneous of degree zero in prices; to ensure that only one solution exists, a price normalization equation, in this case fixing the aggregate consumer price index (CPI), has been added. Hence, all endogenous price changes are relative to CPI.

Data Sources

The bulk of the model data is based on a disaggregated Social Accounting Matrix (SAM) (an 85 × 85 matrix) for 1996/97. This year was selected because it is the same year that IFPRI conducted its EIHS. It was constructed on the basis of data from various official publications including national accounts, government budget, and trade data as well as Egypt's most recent official SAM (Central Bank 1995, 1998; CAPMAS 1996a, 1996b, 1998; IMF 1998). The EIHS and IFPRI research documents based on the EIHS were the primary source for data on household consumption and benefits from food subsidies. Data in Kherallah, Gruhn, and Abdel-Latif (1998) were used for flour production. Information from these and other sources were brought together in one matrix, the disaggregation of which parallels the disaggregation of the current model. Underlying the construction of such a SAM is an attempt to make the best possible use of available scattered data. Inevitably imbalances appear when data from different sources and years are integrated in one framework; a SAM-entropy program, developed at IFPRI, was used to generate a balanced model SAM that retains as much as possible of the information contained in the original data set (Robinson, Cattaneo, and El-Said 1998; Thissen and Löfgren 1998).

For each of the 10 households, the elasticities used for the Almost Ideal Demand System (income and price elasticities for disaggregated foodstuffs and aggregated nonfood consumption) were estimated on the basis of EIHS data, using the Food Characteristics Demand System (Bouis 1996). A variety of sources were used for other elasticity estimates needed for the household nonfood LES functions as well as the functions for import aggregation (Armington), domestic output transformation (CET), production (CES), and (constant elasticity) export demand.[66]

Mathematical Model Structure, Base Run, Validity, and Time Frame

CGE models are typically formulated and solved as systems of simultaneous equations exclusively made up of strict equalities. However, to permit the inclusion of inequality constraints for resource markets and agronomic constraints, the Food CGE model is formulated and solved as a mixed complementarity problem (MCP), consisting of a set of simultaneous equations that are a mix of strict equalities and in-

[66] Consumption elasticities are available on request from the authors. See also Löfgren (1994a).

equalities. The inequalities are linked to bounded (price) variables associated with agricultural resources and labor. The General Algebraic Modeling System (GAMS) software is used both to generate the disaggregated SAM and to implement the model. The model may be solved with Path or Miles, two solvers for mixed complementarity problems.[67]

The base solution of the model is calibrated to exactly replicate the disaggregated 1996/97 SAM. The simulation results indicate the short-run equilibrium responses to changes in policies and exogenous shocks. Each new solution represents a new equilibrium since agents (producers and consumers) have fully adjusted themselves to new prices and incomes. It refers to the short run since capital stocks outside crop agriculture are fixed by sector: the time span is too short for current investment to lead to changes in installed capital or for capital to move between noncrop sectors (see Hazell and Norton 1986).

Tables E.1–E.6 provide additional data and simulation results.

[67] For GAMS, see Brooke, Kendrick, and Meeraus (1988). Rutherford (1995) provides more information on Path and Miles.

Table E.1—Structure of household factor incomes in Social Accounting Matrix (SAM) for 1996–97

	Rural households by quintile					Urban households by quintile				
	1	2	3	4	5	1	2	3	4	5
					(percent)					
Labor	43.9	39.9	31.9	22.5	17.7	56.6	53.8	47.9	35.0	28.3
Agriculture	19.8	16.7	10.4	6.3	4.2	3.1	2.8	2.3	1.3	0.7
Nonagriculture	24.1	23.2	21.5	16.2	13.5	53.5	50.9	45.6	33.8	27.6
Capital	42.6	45.4	51.0	57.8	61.4	41.8	44.6	50.5	63.4	70.1
Agriculture	7.4	8.0	9.2	10.6	11.2	0.9	0.9	0.9	0.9	0.9
Nonagriculture	35.3	37.5	41.8	47.2	50.1	40.9	43.8	49.6	62.4	69.2
Land	13.5	14.7	17.1	19.7	21.0	1.6	1.6	1.6	1.6	1.6
Total	100.0	100.0	100.0	100.0	100.0	100.0	100.0	100.0	100.0	100.0

Source: Model SAM for 1996/97.

Table E.2—Simulation results: Distribution of factor incomes

Factor	Base[a]	Simulations: Targeting oil/sugar subsidy + income tax cut (1)	Wheat-maize flour + transfer to needy (2a)	Wheat-maize flour + transfer to needy + leakage cut (2b)	Wheat-maize flour + transfer to needy + leakage cut + yield increase (2c)	Eliminating oil/sugar subsidy + income tax cut (3)	Targeting total food subsidy + income tax cut (4)	Eliminating total food subsidy + income tax cut (5a)	Eliminating total food subsidy + transfer to needy (5b)
					(percent)				
Agriculture	17.3	0.0	0.1	0.1	0.1	0.0	0.3	0.6	0.7
Labor	4.7	0.0	0.1	0.1	0.0	0.0	0.1	0.2	0.3
Land and capital	12.7	0.0	0.1	0.1	0.1	0.0	0.3	0.4	0.5
Nonagriculture	82.7	0.0	–0.1	–0.1	–0.1	0.0	–0.3	–0.6	–0.7
Labor	27.2	0.0	0.0	0.0	0.1	0.0	–0.1	–0.2	–0.3
Capital	55.5	0.0	–0.1	–0.1	–0.2	0.0	–0.2	–0.4	–0.4
Total	100.0	0.0	0.0	0.0	0.0	0.0	0.0	0.0	0.0

[a] Data in base column show share of total factor income; data for Simulations 1–5b show percentage change from base column figures.

Table E.3—Simulation results: Foreign trade

Factor	Base[a]	Simulations							
		Targeting oil/sugar subsidy + income tax cut (1)	Wheat-maize flour + transfer to needy (2a)	Wheat-maize flour + transfer to needy + leakage cut (2b)	Wheat-maize flour + transfer to needy + leakage cut + yield increase (2c)	Eliminating oil/sugar subsidy + income tax cut (3)	Targeting total food subsidy + income tax cut (4)	Cutting total food subsidy + income tax cut (5a)	Cutting total food subsidy + transfer to needy (5b)
	(million $ at 1996/97 prices)	(percent)							
Food and agriculture									
Net imports	1,962.8	0.0	−6.0	−6.0	−10.9	0.0	−1.8	−1.2	−0.4
Imports	2,333.6	0.0	−5.9	−5.9	−9.3	0.0	−2.6	−2.4	−1.8
Wheat and flour	1,100.4	0.0	−12.7	−12.7	−19.8	0.0	−6.9	−7.1	−5.9
Exports	370.8	0.0	−5.5	−5.5	−0.5	0.1	−6.9	−8.8	−8.9
Other goods and services									
Net imports	161.8	−0.2	72.5	72.4	132.5	0.5	22.3	14.6	4.9
Imports	15,962.0	0.0	0.1	0.1	0.3	0.0	0.0	0.0	0.0
Exports	15,800.0	0.0	−0.7	−0.7	−1.1	0.0	−0.3	−0.3	−0.1

Notes: Changes smaller than 0.05 percent are set at zero. For all simulations, total net imports (the trade deficit) are fixed at $2,124.6 million.

[a] Data for Simulations 1–5b show percentage change from figures in base column.

Table E.4—Simulation results: Real production

Factor	Base[a]	Targeting oil/sugar subsidy + income tax cut (1)	Wheat-maize flour + transfer to needy (2a)	Wheat-maize flour + transfer to needy + leakage cut (2b)	Wheat-maize flour + transfer to needy + leakage cut + yield increase (2c)	Eliminating oil/sugar subsidy + income tax cut (3)	Targeting total food subsidy + income tax cut (4)	Cutting total food subsidy + income tax cut (5a)	Cutting total food subsidy + transfer to needy (5b)
	(billion LE at 1996/97 prices)				(percent)				
Agriculture									
Winter crops									
Wheat	5.1	0.0	–5.3	–5.3	1.0	0.0	–4.1	–9.3	–10.0
Legumes	0.6	0.0	–0.4	–0.4	0.5	–0.1	1.5	2.7	4.2
Long berseem	1.9	0.0	1.5	1.5	1.9	0.0	2.7	3.7	3.8
Short berseem	0.4	0.0	–8.0	–8.0	–7.7	0.0	–7.9	–7.9	–7.9
Winter vegetables	3.0	–0.1	38.5	38.6	–6.9	0.1	22.3	45.9	47.0
Other winter crops	4.8	0.0	0.0	0.0	0.0	0.0	0.8	1.0	1.1
Summer crops									
Cotton	3.2	0.0	–8.0	–8.0	–7.9	0.0	–7.9	–8.0	–8.0
Rice	3.2	0.0	–2.3	–2.3	0.4	0.0	3.4	6.9	7.0

Maize	4.3	0.0	11.6	11.6	11.4	0.0	3.5	4.9	4.9
Summer vegetables	7.1	0.0	−16.1	−16.1	4.3	−0.1	−7.8	−17.3	−17.6
Other summer crops	3.4	0.0	0.0	0.0	0.0	0.0	0.8	1.0	1.1
Perennials									
Fruits	6.1	0.0	−0.2	−0.2	−0.3	0.0	0.1	−0.2	−0.3
Sugarcane	1.2	0.0	0.0	0.0	0.0	0.0	0.8	1.0	1.1
Animal agriculture	17.3	0.0	−0.1	−0.1	0.1	0.0	0.1	−0.1	0.0
Nonagriculture									
Petroleum	19.1	0.0	0.0	0.0	0.0	0.0	0.0	0.0	0.0
Subsidized bread	3.4	0.0	0.7	0.7	−0.3	0.0	−19.5	−29.6	−29.2
Nonsubsidized bread	1.5	0.0	0.3	0.3	0.3	0.0	2.2	2.6	2.8
Subsidized flour	4.1	0.0	0.7	0.7	−0.3	0.0	−15.5	23.3	22.9
Nonsubsidized flour	2.8	0.0	0.3	0.3	0.1	0.0	2.3	3.3	3.4
Other processed food	39.2	0.0	0.0	0.0	0.0	0.0	0.9	1.2	1.3
Cotton ginning	3.9	0.0	−8.0	−8.0	−7.9	0.0	−7.9	−8.0	−8.0
Textiles	30.3	0.0	−0.1	−0.1	0.0	0.0	0.0	−0.1	−0.1
Other industry	56.7	0.0	0.0	0.0	0.0	0.0	0.1	0.1	0.2
Electricity	7.0	0.0	0.0	0.0	0.3	0.0	−0.3	−0.7	−0.5
Construction	33.8	0.0	0.0	0.0	0.0	0.0	−0.1	−0.1	0.0
Government services	25.6	0.0	0.0	0.0	0.0	0.0	0.0	0.0	0.0
Transportation	28.4	0.0	0.0	0.0	0.0	0.0	0.1	0.1	0.0
Other services	119.1	0.0	0.0	0.0	0.0	0.0	0.0	0.1	0.0

[a] Data for Simulations 1–5b show percentage change from figures in base column.

Table E.5—Elasticity values used in the model

Commodity	CET[a]	CES[b]	Export demand	Armington[c]	Intermediate[d]
Winter crops					
Wheat		0.3			0.3
Legumes	0.5	0.3			0.3
Long berseem		0.3			0.3
Short berseem		0.3			0.3
Winter vegetables	0.8	0.3	3.0	0.3	0.3
Other winter crops		0.3			0.3
Summer crops					
Cotton		0.3			0.3
Rice		0.3			0.3
Maize		0.3		1.6	0.3
Summer vegetables	0.8	0.3	3.0	0.3	0.3
Other summer crops		0.3			0.3
Perennials					
Fruits	0.8	0.3		0.3	0.3
Sugarcane		0.3			0.3
Animal agriculture		0.3		0.3	1.2
Nonagriculture					
Petroleum		0.1		2.0	
Subsidized bread		0.6			
Nonsubsidized bread		0.6			
Subsidized flour		0.6			
Nonsubsidized flour		0.6		3.0	
Other processed food	2.0	0.6		0.3	
Cotton ginning		0.6			
Textiles	2.0	0.6		0.3	
Other industry	2.0	0.6		0.3	
Electricity		0.4			
Construction		0.6			
Government services		0.5			
Transportation	2.0	0.6	1.0	0.3	
Other services	2.0	0.6	1.0	0.3	

Note: For a brief survey of elasticities of CGE models, see Löfgren (1994a).

[a] Elasticity of transformation between exports and domestic sales in Constant Elasticity of Transformation (CET) function.

[b] Elasticity of factor substitution in Constant Elasticity of Substitution (CES) value-added functions.

[c] Elasticity of substitution between imports and domestic goods in CES aggregation function.

[d] Elasticity of substitution between intermediate inputs in agriculture.

Table E.6—Mathematical statement for the Egypt Food CGE model[a,b]

Sets			
$\alpha \in A$	Activities	$z \in Z$	Institutions [households, government (= *gov*), rest of the world (= *row*)] and factors
$\alpha \in ACR\ (\subset A)$	Crop activities	$f \in F\ (\subset Z)$	Factors [labor and capital factors, land-water (= *l–w*)]
$c \in C$	Disaggregated commodities	$f \in FSUB$	Subfactors (summer and winter land, water)
$c \in CF$	Disaggregated food and nonfood aggregate	$t \in I\ (\subset Z)$	Domestic institutions (households and government)
$c \in CNF\ (\subset C)$	Disaggregated nonfood	$h \in H\ (\subset I)$	Households
Parameters			
cpi	Consumer price index	qg_c	Government consumption
$cwts_c$	Weight of commodity *c* in consumer price index	$qinv_c$	Fixed investment demand for *c*
$fsav$	Foreign savings (foreign currency)	$shrgdp_{h,gov}$	Nominal GDP share transferred from government to household *h*
$gsav$	Government savings	$shry_{if}$	Share of domestic institution *i* in income of factor *f*
ica_{ca}	Intermediate input *c* per unit of activity *a*	ta_a	Indirect tax rates for activity *a*
ife_{fa}	Quantity of subfactor *f* per unit of land-water aggregate for activity *a*	tm_c	Import tariff rate (including sales tax)
mps_h	Share of post-tax income of household *h* to savings	tq_c	Rate of sales tax
pwe_c	World price of exports (foreign currency)	$tr_{zz}{}^{t}$	Transfer to institution/factor *z* from institution/factor *z′*
pwm_c	World price of imports (foreign currency)	$trsub_{x,gov}$	Subsidy transfer to institution/factor z (for rationed commodity or leakage)
$qdst_c$	Stock change for commodity *c*	ty_h	Direct tax rate for household *h*
qfs_f	Supply of factor *f*	γ_{ac}	Yield of commodity *c* per unit of activity *a*
$qfssub_f$	Supply of subfactor *f*	σ_c	Rate of household consumption subsidy for commodity *c*
Variables			
EG	Government expenditures	QF_{ts}	Demand for factor *f* from activity *a*
EH_h	Household consumption expenditures	$QFSUB_{fa}$	Demand for subfactor *f* from activity *a*
EXR	Exchange rate (units of foreign currency per unit of domestic currency)	QH_{ch}	Consumption demand for *c* from household *h*
GDP	Nominal GDP at market prices	$QINT_c$	Intermediate input demand for *c*
PA_a	Output revenue per unit of activity *a*	QM_c	Imports of *c*
PD_c	Price of domestic output sold domestically	QQ_c	Supply of composite commodity *c*

(continued)

Table E.6—Continued

Variables *(continued)*

PE_c	Price of exports	QX_c	Total output of commodity *c*
PM_c	Price of imports	W_f	Wage of factor *f*
PQ_c	Price of composite good	$WFDIST_{fa}$	Wage distortion factor
PVA_a	Activity value-added (net) price	$WFSUB_f$	Wage of subfactor
PX_c	Average producer price for commodity *c*	YF_t	Income of factor *f*
QA_a	Level of activity *a*	YG	Government income
QD_c	Domestic sales of domestic output	YIF_{it}	Income of domestic institution *i* from factor *f*
QE_c	Exports	YH_h	Income of household *h*

Functions[c]

CES*	Constant elasticity of substitution	LES*	Linear expenditure system
CET*	Constant elasticity of transformation	AIDS*	Almost ideal demand system

Equations

Number	Equation	Domain	Description
Price block			
1	$PM_c = pwm_c \cdot (1 + tm_c) \cdot EXR$	$c \in C$	Import price in domestic currency
2	$PE_c = pwe_c \cdot EXR$	$c \in C$	Export price in domestic currency
3	$PQ_c = \frac{(PD_c \cdot QD_c + PM_c \cdot QM_c)}{QQ_c}(1 + tq_c)$	$c \in C$	Average demand price of composite commodity
4	$PX_c = \frac{(PD_c \cdot QD_c + PE_c \cdot QE_c)}{QX_c}$	$c \in C$	Average producer price of commodity *c*
5	$PA_a = \sum_{c \in C} \gamma_{ac} \cdot PX_c$	$a \in A$	Gross activity price (=unit revenue)
6	$PVA_a = PA_a \cdot (1 - ta_a) - \sum_{c \in C} ica_{ca} \cdot PQ_c$	$a \in A$	Activity value added (net) price
7	$WF_{1-w} \cdot WFDIST_{1-w,a} = \sum_{f \in FSUB} ifa_{fa} \cdot WFSUB_f$	$a \in ACR$	Land-water rent by crop activity
Supply and trade block[d]			
8	$QA_a = CES[QF_{fa}]$	$a \in A$	Level of production activity
9	$QF_{ta} = CES^*[W_t \cdot WFDIST_{fa}, PVA_a]$	$f \in F$ $a \in A$	Demand for factor *f* from activity *a*
10	$QINT_c = \sum_{a \in A} ica_{ca} \cdot QA_a$	$c \in C$	Intermediate input demand
11	$QFSUB_{fa} = ifa_{fa} \cdot QF_{l-w,a}$	$f \in FSUB$ $a \in ACR$	Demand for subfactor *f* from crop activity *a*
12	$QX_c = \sum_{a \in A} \gamma_{ac} \cdot QA_a$	$c \in C$	Output of commodity *c*

(continued)

Table E.6—Continued

Equations *(continued)*

Number	Equation	Domain	Description
13	$QX_c = CET[QE_c, QD_c]$	$c_{206}C$	Function transforming output to exports and domestic sales
14	$\frac{QE_c}{QD_c} = CET^*\left[\frac{PE_c}{PD_c}\right]$	$c \in C$	First-order Condition (FOC) for output transformation
15	$QQ_c = CES[QM_c, QD_c]$	$c \in C$	Function aggregating imports and domestic sales to composite supply
16	$\frac{QM_c}{QD_c} = CES^*\left[\frac{PD_c}{PM_c}\right]$	$c \in C$	FOC for commodity aggregation
Institution block			
17	$YF_f = \sum_{a \in A} W_f \cdot WFDIST_{fa} \cdot QF_{fa} + trsub_{f,gov}$	$f \in F$	Income of factor *f*
18	$YIF_{if} = shry_{if}(YF_f - tr_{row,f} \cdot EXR)$	$i \in I$ $f \in F$	Income of domestic institution *i* from factor *f*
19	$YH_h = \sum_{f \in F} YIF_{hf} + shrgdp_{h,gov} \cdot GDP$ $+ tr_{h,row} \cdot EXR + trsub_{h,gov}$	$h \in H$	Household income
20	$EH_h = (1 - mps_h) \cdot (1 = ty_h) \cdot$ $YH_h - tr_{row,h} \cdot EXR$	$h \in H$	Household consumption expenditure
21	$QH_{ch} = AIDS^*[(1 - \sigma_c) \cdot PQ_c, EH_h]$	$c \in CF$ $h \in H$	Household consumption demand for disaggregated food and aggregated nonfood
22	$PQ_{n-f=} LES^*[(1 - \sigma_{cnf)} . PQ_{cnf}]$		Consumer price index for nonfood
23	$QH_{ch} = LES^*[(1 - \sigma_{c)} . PQ_c, PQ_{n-f} . QH_{n-f,h]}$	$c \in CNF$ $h \in H$	Household consumption demand for disaggregated nonfood
24	$YG = YIF_{gov,f} + \sum_{h \in H} ty_h \cdot YH_h$ $+ \sum_{c \in C} tq_c \cdot (PD_c \cdot QD_c + PM_c \cdot QM_c)$ $+ \sum_{a \in A} ta_a \cdot PA_a \cdot QA_a + \sum_{c \in C} tm_c \cdot pwm_c \cdot QM_c$ $+ tr_{gov,row}$		Government income
25	$EG = \sum_{c \in C} PQ_c \cdot qg_c + \sum_{h \in H} shrgdp_{h,gov} \cdot GDP$ $+ tr_{row,gov} \cdot EXR + \sum_{c \in C} \sum_{h \in H} \sigma_c \cdot PQ_c \cdot QH_{ch} + \sum_{z \in Z} trsub_{z,gov}$		Government expenditure
26	$GDP = \sum_{c \in C} \sum_{h \in H} PQ_c \cdot (1 - \sigma_c) \cdot QH_{ch} + \sum_{c \in C} PQ_c \cdot qinv_c$ $+ \sum_{c \in C} PQ_c \cdot qdst_c + \sum_{c \in C} PQ_c \cdot qg_c$ $+ \sum_{c \in C} pwe_c \cdot QE_c \cdot EXR - \sum_{c \in C} pwm_c \cdot QM_c \cdot EXR$		Nominal GDP

(continued)

Table E.6—Continued

Equations *(continued)*

Number	Equation	Domain	Description
System constraint block			
27	$QQ_c = QINT_c + \sum_{h \in H} QH_{ch} + qg_c + qinv_c + qdst_c$	$c \cdot \in C$	Market equilibrium for composite commodity ($S = D$)
28	$qfs_f = \sum_{a \in A} QF_{fa}$	$f \in F$ $f \neq l - w$	Market equilibrium for factors ($S = D$)
29	$qfssub_f \geq \sum_{a \in ACR} QFSUB_{fa}$ $[WFSUB_f \geq 0]$	$f \in FSUB$	Market equilibrium for subfactors ($S \geq D$)
30	$\sum_{c \in C} pwm_c \cdot QM_c + \sum_{z \in Z} tr_{row,z} = \sum_{c \in C} pwe_c \cdot QE_c + \sum_{z \in Z} tr_{z,row} + fsav$		Current account balance (in foreign currency)
31	$gsav = YG - EG$		Government savings constraint
32	$\sum_{h \in H} mps_h \cdot (1 - ty_h) \cdot YH_h + gsav + EXR \cdot fsav = \sum_{c \in C} PQ_c \cdot (qinv_c + qdst_c)$		Savings-investment balance
33	$cpi = \sum_{c \in C} cwts_c \cdot (1 - \sigma_c) \cdot PQ_c$		Consumer price index (numéraire)

[a] The following notational convention is used: Subscripts are set indices. Variables are written with upper-case Latin letters. Parameters appear as Greek letters or as lower-case Latin letters.

[b] The mathematical statement is simplified; the text in this Appendix gives a fuller description. The following aspects have been suppressed: (1) perfect substitutability/transformability between exports, imports, and domestic output for selected commodities (in place of imperfect substitutability/transformability); (2) constant-elasticity demand curves for selected export commodities (in place of fixed foreign-currency export price); (3) domain controls (limiting equations and variables to subsets of the sets indicated); (4) price-responsiveness of selected intermediate input coefficients; (5) agronomic constraints; (6) flexing of subsidy rate and fixing of total consumer price, $(1 - \sigma_c) \cdot PQ_c$, for subsidized commodities with a fixed consumer price.

[c] CES*, CET*, AIDS*, and LES* indicate relationships derived from the respective functions. In general, WF is flexible and WFDIST is fixed. Exceptions include the aggregate land-water factor (for which WF is fixed while WFDIST is flexible for all land-water crop activity pairs), and factors or activities with special treatment (activity-specific capital for noncrop activities and special assumptions for the oil and electricity activities).

[d] Complementary constraints are shown in brackets in the equation column.

APPENDIX F

Supplementary Tables

Table F.1—Imported and domestic wheat supplied through the subsidy system

Year	Imported wheat	Domestically procured wheat	Total	Per capita subsidized wheat
	(1,000 tons)	(1,000 metric tons)		(kilograms/year)
1991/92	5,532	614	6,146	110.7
1992/93	4,848	1,042	5,891	103.5
1993/94	4,071	936	5,007	85.9
1994/95	4,936	1,123	6,059	101.7
1995/96	5,542	1,252	6,795	111.6
1996/97	4,768	1,205	5,973	96.3
1997/98	5,210	1,525	6,735	106.3

Source: Unpublished data, Ministry of Trade and Supply.

Table F.2—Total domestic production and imports of cooking oil, and supply of subsidized cooking oil

Year	Domestic production	Imports	Subsidized cooking oil	Per capita subsidized cooking oil
		(1,000 metric tons)		(kilograms/year)
1991/92	103	485	260	4.7
1992/93	80	530	277	4.9
1993/94	55	555	242	4.2
1994/95	48	550	235	3.9
1995/96	55	553	221	3.6
1996/97	58	550	220	3.5
1997/98	62	548	230	3.6

Source: Unpublished data, Ministry of Trade and Supply.

Table F.3—Total domestic production and imports of sugar, and supply of subsidized sugar

Year	Domestic production	Imports	Subsidized sugar	Per capita subsidized sugar
		(1,000 metric tons)		(kilograms/year)
1991/92	1,089	544	872	15.7
1992/93	1,100	249	854	15.0
1993/94	1,214	393	850	14.6
1994/95	1,210	491	721	12.1
1995/96	1,189	536	620	10.2
1996/97	1,110	585	590	9.5
1997/98	1,200	500	585	9.2

Source: Unpublished data, Ministry of Trade and Supply.
Note: Since 1991/92, all subsidized sugar has been procured from domestic production.

Table F.4—Distribution of bakeries producing subsidized *baladi* bread, by governorates, 1997

	Number of bakeries			Number of bakeries per 100,000 population[a]		
Governorate	Urban	Rural	Total	Urban	Rural	Total
			(1,000 metric tons)			
Metropolitan	2,567		2,567	23		23
Cairo	1,480		1,480	22		22
Alexandria	860		860	26		26
Port Said	130		130	28		28
Suez	97		97	23		23
Lower Egypt	2,704	1,544	4,248	38	8	16
Damietta	138	72	210	55	11	23
Dakahlia	457	183	640	39	6	15
Sharkia	395	258	653	41	8	15
Kalyoubia	417	299	716	31	15	22
Kafr El-Sheikh	202	77	279	40	4	13
Gharbia	380	111	491	36	5	14
Menoufia	245	184	429	45	8	16
Behera	281	320	601	31	10	15
Ismailia	189	40	229	55	11	32
Upper Egypt	2,049	1,431	3,480	30	10	16
Giza	496	258	754	19	12	16
Beni-Suef	140	113	253	32	8	14
Fayoum	190	86	276	43	6	14
Menia	420	420	840	65	16	25
Assyout	230	210	440	30	10	16
Suhag	292	162	454	43	7	15
Quena	171	119	290	33	6	12
Luxor	25	0	25	7	0	7
Aswan	85	63	148	20	11	15
Frontier	276	122	398	55	38	49
Red Sea	50	22	72	36	128	46
Matrouh	55	28	83	49	28	39
El Wadi El Guedid	21	11	32	31	15	23
North Sinai	130	55	185	87	53	73
South Sinai	20	6	26	68	24	48
Egypt total	7,596	3,097	10,693	30	9	18

Source: Unpublished data, Ministry of Trade and Supply.

[a] The 1996 census population data are used (see Table F.7).

Table F.5—Distribution of total quantity of subsidized wheat flour, by governorates, 1997

	Flour to bakeries			Flour to warehouses		
Governorate	Urban	Rural	Total	Urban	Rural	Total
			(1,000 metric tons)			
Metropolitan	1,190.3		1,190.3	15.8		15.8
Cairo	819.4		819.4	0.0		0.0
Alexandria	298.2		298.2	12.9		12.9
Port Said	39.0		39.0	0.9		0.9
Suez	33.7		33.7	2.0		2.0
Lower Egypt	838.2	264.3	11,02.6	69.8	255.8	325.6
Damietta	44.5	17.3	61.8	3.8	40.2	44.0
Dakahlia	115.5	30.9	146.4	2.0	6.8	8.8
Sharkia	149.2	32.6	181.1	0.0	0.2	0.2
Kalyoubia	142.9	83.7	226.6	0.6	9.3	9.9
Kafr El-Sheikh	34.2	5.8	40.0	3.8	39.1	43.0
Gharbia	122.5	20.3	142.8	18.2	28.0	46.2
Menoufia	88.6	36.0	124.6	20.9	69.2	90.1
Behera	92.6	31.8	124.4	20.5	50.2	70.7
Ismailia	48.3	5.9	54.2	...	12.7	12.7
Upper Egypt	732.7	343.4	1,076.1	253.7	628.5	882.2
Giza	226.1	129.5	355.6	0	85.0	85.0
Beni-Suef	70.8	22.5	93.3	5.0	9.5	14.5
Fayoum	52.8	26.5	79.3	27.8	63.9	91.7
Menia	118.5	83.0	201.5	1.0	0.1	1.1
Assyout	88.2	32.2	120.4	45.9	68.0	113.9
Suhag	68.8	25.3	94.1	53.0	169.0	222.0
Quena	52.6	16.9	69.5	58.3	168.5	226.8
Luxor	14.9	0	14.9	34.1	0	34.1
Aswan	40.0	7.5	47.5	28.6	64.5	93.1
Frontier	49.5	6.0	55.5	18.6	13.0	31.6
Red Sea	15.2	0.5	15.7	4.5	1.5	6.0
Matrouh	14.6	1.9	16.5	4.0	0.4	4.4
El Wadi El Guedid	2.9	2.3	5.2	0.85	2.4	3.2
North Sinai	10.4	1.2	11.6	7.8	7.9	15.0
South Sinai	6.4	0.1	6.5	2.1	0.9	3.0
Egypt total	2,810.8	613.7	3,424.5	358.0	897.2	1,255.2

Source: Unpublished data, Ministry of Trade and Supply.

Table F.6—Distribution of total quantity of subsidized sugar and cooking oil, by governorates, 1997

	Sugar			Cooking oil		
Governorate	Urban	Rural	Total	Urban	Rural	Total
			(1,000 metric tons)			
Metropolitan	116.9		116.9	55.3		55.3
Cairo	77.3		77.3	34.8		34.8
Alexandria	32.0		32.0	17.2		17.2
Port Said	4.0		4.0	2.1		2.1
Suez	3.6		3.6	1.2		1.2
Lower Egypt	101.1	131.2	232.3	24.6	47.9	72.5
Damietta	3.3	6.3	9.6	1.2	2.5	3.7
Dakahlia	15.3	24.0	39.3	4.5	8.7	13.2
Sharkia	12.3	15.8	28.1	2.7	4.5	7.2
Kalyoubia	11.2	14.0	25.2	3.5	5.5	9.0
Kafr El-Sheikh	10.0	11.5	21.5	3.0	4.9	7.9
Gharbia	12.0	20.5	32.5	2.3	7.5	9.8
Menoufia	25.4	23.0	48.4	3.2	4.3	7.5
Behera	9.0	12.5	21.5	2.9	8.5	11.4
Ismailia	2.6	3.6	6.2	1.3	1.5	2.8
Upper Egypt	72.3	58.4	130.7	27.7	22.7	50.4
Giza	20.2	3.5	23.7	10.3	4.5	14.8
Beni-Suef	1.2	0.1	1.26	0.4	0.02	0.4
Fayoum	12.2	6.0	18.2	3.5	1.7	5.2
Menia	6.7	14.2	20.9	2.3	6.0	8.3
Assyout	12.3	12.1	24.4	1.9	2.0	3.9
Suhag	1.3	1.5	2.8	3.0	2.5	5.5
Quena	10.9	13.5	24.4	3.5	4.5	8.0
Luxor	1.0	0.0	1.0	0.5	0.0	0.5
Aswan	6.5	7.5	14.0	2.3	1.5	3.8
Frontier	6.6	2.6	9.1	2.5	0.7	3.3
Red Sea	0.9	0.1	1.0	0.5	0.03	0.5
Matrouh	1.5	1.3	2.8	1.0	0.3	1.3
El Wadi El Guedid	2.1	0.5	2.6	0.3	0.2	0.5
North Sinai	1.9	0.6	2.5	0.6	0.2	0.8
South Sinai	0.2	0.03	0.2	0.1	0.02	0.1
Egypt total	296.9	192.1	489.0	110.1	71.4	181.5

Source: Unpublished data, Ministry of Trade and Supply.

Table F.7—Population living in Egypt, by governorates, 1996 census

Governorate	Population		
	Urban	Rural	Total
Cairo	6,789,479		6,789,479
Alexandria	3,328,196		3,328,196
Port Said	469,533		469,533
Suez	417,610		417,610
Damietta	251,087	663,527	914,614
Dakahlia	1,175,333	3,048,322	4,223,655
Sharkia	968,460	3,319,388	4,287,848
Kalyoubia	1,345,967	1,956,893	3,302,860
Kafr El-Sheikh	509,774	1,713,146	2,222,920
Gharbia	1,057,152	2,347,675	3,404,827
Menoufia	548,814	2,209,685	2,758,499
Behera	910,896	3,070,313	3,981,209
Ismailia	340,737	374,272	715,009
Giza	2,590,357	2,189,508	4,779,865
Beni-Suef	437,840	1,422,340	1,860,180
Fayoum	446,972	1,542,909	1,989,881
Menia	642,957	2,665,918	3,308,875
Assyout	763,431	2,038,754	2,802,185
Suhag	684,046	2,438,954	3,123,000
Quena	517,320	1,924,100	2,441,420
Luxor	360,503	0	360,503
Aswan	416,804	556,867	973,671
Red Sea	138,571	17,124	155,695
Matrouh	112,398	99,468	211,866
El-Wadi El-Guedid	68,419	73,318	141,737
North Sinai	149,143	103,607	252,750
South Sinai	29,323	25,172	54,495
Egypt total	25,471,122	33,801,260	59,272,382

Source: Central Authority for Public Mobilization and Statistics (CAPMAS), 1996 census.

Notes: Egypt's total population stood at 61,452,382 on December 31, 1996. Of the total, 59,272,382 lived in Egypt, while 2,180,000 lived abroad as temporary migrants.

Table F.8—Distribution of ration cards, 1981/82–1997/98

Year	Green cards	Red cards	Total
	(number of ration cards in thousands)		
1981/82	8,216	238	8,454
1982/83	8,427	244	8,671
1983/84	8,643	251	8,894
1984/85	8,865	257	9,122
1985/86	9,095	264	9,359
1986/87	9,277	267	9,444
1987/88	9,663	271	9,934
1988/89	9,906	283	10,189
1989/90	10,222	317	10,539
1990/91	10,507	315	10,822
1991/92	10,560	309	10,869
1992/93	10,429	304	10,733
1993/94	9,827	276	10,103
1994/95	9,808	279	10,087
1995/96	9,739	285	10,024
1996/97	9,650	293	9,943
1997/98	9,580	301	9,881

Source: Unpublished data, Ministry of Trade and Supply.

Table F.9—Cost-effectiveness of Egyptian food subsidies for consumers, 1997

Item	Flour-equivalent *baladi* bread	Wheat flour	Sugar	Cooking oil
Total quantity (1,000 metric tons)	3,416.04	1,253.64	590.00	220.00
Total costs of subsidy (million LE)	2,307.8	558.6	489.5	384.7
Unit costs of subsidy (LE/metric ton)	675.58	445.58	829.66	1,748.64
Unit value of subsidy to consumers (LE/metric ton)	660.04	416.35	812.49	1,172.37
System leakage (percent)	11.8	27.8	19.6	15.4
Income transfer to all consumers (LE/metric ton)	582.16	300.60	653.24	991.83
Cost/income transfer to all consumers (LE)	1.16	1.48	1.27	1.76
Benefits to nonneedy (percent)	61	60	62	62
Income transfer to needy (LE/metric ton)	227.04	120.24	248.23	376.89
Cost/income transfer to needy (LE)	2.98	3.71	3.34	4.64

Source: Calculated by the authors using data from the IFPRI Food Security Research Project in Egypt, "Egypt Integrated Household Survey, 1997," and the Ministry of Trade and Supply.

References

Ahluwalia, D. 1993. Public distribution of food in India: Coverage, targeting and leakages. *Food Policy* 18(1): 33–54.

Ahmed, A. U. 1992. *Operational performance of the rural rationing program in Bangladesh.* Working Papers on Bangladesh 5. Washington, D.C.: International Food Policy Research Institute.

Ahmed, A. U., and K. Billah. 1994. *Food for education program in Bangladesh: An early assessment.* Manuscript No. 62. Dhaka: International Food Policy Research Institute. Mimeo.

Ahmed, A. U., and H. E. Bouis. 1998. A review of international experience on food subsidy programs: Lessons learned for Egypt. A report of the Food Security Research Project in Egypt. International Food Policy Research Institute, Washington, D.C.

Ahmed, A. U., H. E. Bouis, A. R. Hegazy, and A. A. Ganainy. 1999. The application of proxy means testing to determine eligibility for ration card food subsidies in Egypt. A report of the Food Security Research Project in Egypt. International Food Policy Research Institute, Washington, D.C.

Alderman, H. 1986. Food subsidies and state policies in Egypt. In *Food, states and peasants: Analyses of the agrarian question in the Middle East,* ed. A. Richards. Boulder, Colo., U.S.A.: Westview Press.

———. 1991. Food subsidies and the poor. In *Essays on poverty, equity and growth,* ed. George Psacharopoulos. Washington, D.C.: World Bank.

Alderman, H., and J. von Braun. 1984. *The effects of the Egyptian food ration and subsidy system on income distribution and consumption.* Research Report 45. Washington, D.C.: International Food Policy Research Institute.

Alderman, H., J. von Braun, and S. A. Sakr. 1982. *Egypt's food subsidy and rationing system: A description.* Research Report 34. Washington, D.C.: International Food Policy Research Institute.

Alderman, H., M. G. Chaudhry, and M. Garcia. 1988. *Household food security in Pakistan: The ration shop system.* Working Papers on Food Subsidies. Washington, D.C.: International Food Policy Research Institute.

Ali, A. I. 1991. The demand analysis of cereal products: Various econometric techniques. *Egyptian Journal of Agricultural Economics* 6 (1): 1–20.

Ali, S. M., and R. H. Adams, Jr. 1996. The Egyptian food subsidy system: Operation and effects on income distribution. *World Development* 24 (11): 1777–1791.

Amin, G. A. 1995. *Egypt's economic predicament.* New York: E. J. Brill.

Ayaad, A. 1994. *Estimation of final consumption for the years 1986/87–1993/94 and expenditure elasticities based on the household survey of 1990/91.* Report (Arabic). Cairo: Ministry of National Planning.

Badiane, O., M. Kherallah, and A. Abdel-Latif. 1998. Evolution of wheat policy reform in Egypt and adjustment of local markets. A report of the Food Security Research Project in Egypt. International Food Policy Research Institute, Washington, D.C.

Balisacan, A. M. 1994. *Design of a poverty-targeted food subsidy program in the Philippines.* A policy paper prepared for the Agribusiness System Assistance Program (ASAP). Quezon City: University of the Philippines.

Bouis, H. 1994. The effect of income on demand for food in poor countries: Are our databases giving us reliable estimates? *Journal of Development Economics* 44 (June): 199–226.

———. 1996. A food demand system based on demand for characteristics: If there is "curvature" in the Slutsky matrix, what do the curves look like and why? *Journal of Development Economics* 51 (December): 239–266.

Bouis, H., A. U. Ahmed, and A. S. Hamza. 1999. Patterns of food consumption and nutrition in Egypt. A report of the Food Security Research Project in Egypt. International Food Policy Research Institute, Washington, D.C.

Bouis, H., and L. Haddad. 1992. Are estimates of calorie-income elasticities too high? A recalibration of the plausible range. *Journal of Development Economics* 39 (December): 333–364.

Braun, J. von. 1981. A demand system for Egypt—Estimation results and scenario analysis for alternative food price policies. International Food Policy Research Institute, Washington, D.C.

Brooke, A., D. Kendrick, and A. Meeraus. 1988. *GAMS: A user's guide.* Redwood, Calif., U.S.A.: Scientific Press.

CAPMAS (Central Agency for Public Mobilization and Statistics). 1996a. *Statistical yearbook.* June. Cairo.

———. 1996b. Harakat al-Intaj wat-Tijara al-Kharijiyya wal-Istihlak li-Ba'd as-Sila' hatta 'am 1994/95 (Production, Foreign Trade, and Consumption of Selected Commodities until 1994/95). June.

Cardiff, P. W. 1997. *The 1995/1996 household income, expenditure and consumption survey: Final analysis report.* Washington, D.C.: U.S. Agency for International Development (USAID)/Egypt and U.S. Bureau of the Census.

Cassandra. 1995. The impending crisis in Egypt. *Middle East Journal* 49 (1): 9–27.

Central Bank of Egypt. 1995. *Annual report, 1994–95.* Cairo.

———. 1998. *Annual report, 1997–98.* Cairo.

Clarke, D. L. 1997. U.S. security assistance to Egypt and Israel: Politically untouchable? *Middle East Journal* 51 (2). Available at http://www2.ari.net/mei /clark.htm.

Datt, G., D. Jolliffe, and M. Sharma. 1998. A profile of poverty in Egypt: 1997. A report of the Food Security Research Project in Egypt. International Food Policy Research Institute, Washington, D.C.

Deaton, A., and J. Muellbauer. 1980. *Economics and consumer behavior.* New York: Cambridge University Press.

Dervis, K., J. de Melo, and S. Robinson. 1982. *General equilibrium models for development policy.* New York: Cambridge University Press.

Egypt—Ministry of Agriculture. 1998. *al-Iqtisad az-zira'i.* Publication from the Economic Affairs Sector. Cairo.

FAO (Food and Agriculture Organization of the United Nations). 1982. Food composition tables for the Near East. Rome.

Fayyad, B. S., R. Johnson and M. El Kishin. 1995. *Consumer demand for major foods in Egypt.* Working Paper 95-WP 138. Ames, Iowa, U.S.A.: Center of Agricultural and Rural Development, Iowa State University.

Garcia, M., and P. Pinstrup-Andersen. 1987. *The pilot food price subsidy scheme in the Philippines: Its impact on income, food consumption, and nutritional status.* Research Report 61. Washington, D.C.: International Food Policy Research Institute.

Grosh, M. E. 1994. *Administering targeted social programs in Latin America: From platitudes to practice.* Washington, D.C.: World Bank.

Gutner, T., S. Gomaa, and S. Nasser 1998. The political economy of food subsidy reform in Egypt. A report of the Food Security Research Project in Egypt. International Food Policy Research Institute, Washington, D.C.

Harrison, K. M. 1996. Agricultural processing, marketing and trade in the reform era. In *Egypt's agriculture in a reform era,* ed. L. B. Fletcher. Ames, Iowa, U.S.A.: Iowa State University Press.

Hazell, P. B. R., and R. D. Norton. 1986. *Mathematical programming for economic analysis in agriculture.* New York: Macmillan.

Ibrahim, M. 1988. *Estimation of a demand system for households in Egypt.* Report #1482. (Arabic). Cairo: Institute of National Planning.

Ibrahim, S. E., and H. Löfgren. 1996. *Successful adjustment and declining governance? The case of Egypt.* World Bank Private Sector Development Department Essays on Governance, Leadership and Communication. Washington, D.C.: World Bank.

IMF (International Monetary Fund). 1998. *International financial statistics yearbook.* Washington, D.C.

INP (Institute of National Planning). 1996. *Egypt human development report 1996.* Nasr City, Cairo.

Khalil, M. 1999. Economics of maize in Egypt. International Food Policy Research Institute, Washington, D.C., and the Food Security Research Unit of the Agricultural Policy Reform Program in Egypt in collaboration with the Ministry of Agriculture and Land Reclamation, and the Ministry of Trade and Supply, Cairo.

Kherallah, M., P. Gruhn, and A. Abdel-Latif. 1998. The wheat milling sector in Egypt: Structure, performance, and future prospects. A report of the Food Security Research Project in Egypt. International Food Policy Research Institute, Washington, D.C.

Kherallah, M., H. Löfgren, P. Gruhn, and M. Reeder. 2000. Wheat policy reform in Egypt: Adjustment of local markets and options for future reforms. IFPRI Research Report No. 115. International Food Policy Research Institute, Washington, D.C.

Khouri-Dager, N. 1996. The state, urban households, and management of daily life: Food and social order in Cairo. In *Development, change, and gender in Cairo,* ed. D. Singerman and H. Hoodfar. Bloomington, Ind.: Indiana University Press.

Löfgren, H. 1994a. A brief survey of elasticities for CGE models. Paper presented to the Ford Foundation. December. Washington, D.C.

———. 1994b. Egypt's experience from CGE modeling: A critical review. *L'Egypte Contemporaine* 85 (437–438): 33–58.

Löfgren, H., and M. Kherallah. 1998. A general equilibrium analysis of alternative wheat policy scenarios for Egypt. Egypt Food Security Project Paper No. 2. International Food Policy Research Institute, Washington, D.C.

Mesilhy, M. A. 1980. Demand for food in Egypt. M.A. thesis. Faculty of Agriculture, Zagazig University, Egypt.

Pinstrup-Andersen, P., N. R. de Londono, and E. Hoover. 1976. The impact of increasing food supply on human nutrition: Implications for commodity priorities in agricultural research and policy. *American Journal of Agricultural Economics* 58 (2): 131–142.

Rajagopalan, R. 1989. *Indian sugar economy: Policy issues and impacts.* Research Paper No. 6. Anand: Indian Institute of Rural Management.

Robinson, S., and K. Thierfelder. 1999. A note on taxes, prices, wages, and welfare in general equilibrium models. Trade and Macroeconomics Division Discussion Paper 39. International Food Policy Research Institute, Washington, D.C.

Robinson, S., A. Cattaneo, and M. El-Said. 1998. Estimating a social accounting matrix using cross entropy methods. Trade and Macroeconomics Division Discussion Paper 33. International Food Policy Research Institute, Washington, D.C.

Rutherford, T. 1995. Extensions of GAMS for complementarity problems arising in applied economic analysis. *Journal of Economic Dynamics and Control* 19 (8): 1299–1324.

Sadowski, Y. M. 1991. *Political vegetables? Businessman and bureaucrat in the development of Egyptian agriculture.* Washington, D.C.: Brookings Institution.

Scobie, G. 1981. *Government policy and food imports: The case of wheat in Egypt.* Research Report 29. Washington, D.C.: International Food Policy Research Institute.

Seddon, D. 1986. Politics and the price of bread in Tunisia. In *Food, states and peasants: Analyses of the agrarian question in the Middle East,* ed. A. Richards. Boulder, Colo., U.S.A.: Westview Press.

Shalaby, F. 1978. A report on wheat consumption in Egypt. U.S. Agency for International Development (USAID)/Egypt, Cairo.

Singerman, D. 1995. *Avenues of participation: Family, politics, and networks in urban quarters of Cairo.* Princeton, N.J., U.S.A.: Princeton University Press.

Subbarao, K., A. U. Ahmed, and T. Teklu. 1996. *Selected social safety net programs in the Philippines: Targeting, cost-effectiveness, and options for reform.* Discussion Paper 317. Washington, D.C.: World Bank.

Thissen, M., and H. Löfgren. 1998. A new approach to SAM updating with an application to Egypt. *Environment and Planning Series A* 30 (11): 1991–2003.

Tuck, L., and K. Lindert. 1996. *From universal food subsidies to a self-targeted program: A case study in Tunisian reform.* Discussion Paper 351. Washington, D.C.: World Bank.

USDA (U.S. Department of Agriculture), Foreign Agricultural Service (FAS). 1999. Grain: World markets and trade. Available at http://www.fas.usda.gov/grain-arc.htm.

WGTFI (Working Group on Targeted Food Interventions). 1994. Options for targeting food interventions in Bangladesh. Report prepared by WGTFI, chaired by IFPRI. International Food Policy Research Institute, Washington, D.C.

World Bank. 1984. *Nutrition review.* Population, Health, and Nutrition Department. Washington, D.C.

———. 1995. *Arab Republic of Egypt. Social welfare study (strengthening the social safety net).* Report No. 13858-EGT. Washington, D.C.

———. 1997. *Country assistance strategy for the Arab Republic of Egypt.* Report 16533-EGT. Washington, D.C.

Zimmerman, R. F. 1993. *Dollars, diplomacy and dependency: Dilemmas of U.S. economic aid.* Boulder, Colo., U.S.A.: Lynne Rienner Publishers.

About the Authors

Akhter U. Ahmed is a senior research fellow in IFPRI's Food Consumption and Nutrition Division. He works on strategies for restructuring social safety net programs to improve the food security and nutrition of the poor, and on poverty monitoring in developing countries.

Howarth E. Bouis is a senior research fellow in IFPRI's Food Consumption and Nutrition Division. He directs the micronutrients project of the CGIAR, which focuses on breeding for micronutrient-dense staple food crops and understanding how programs and policies can be modified to improve the diets of poor people in developing countries.

Tamar Gutner, a visiting researcher at IFPRI during the study, is assistant professor of international relations at American University's School of International Service.

Hans Löfgren is a senior research fellow in IFPRI's Trade and Macroeconomics Division. He leads IFPRI's team on macroeconomic policies, rural development, and household food security. His research focuses on the effects of structural adjustment policies on poverty, the agricultural sector, and the macroeconomy.

Made in the USA
Monee, IL
08 November 2026

67984629R00090